100 favourite
20 minute
dishes

PHOTOGRAPHY BY LINDSAY KEATS

CW00404585

Published by Hyndman Publishing,
PO Box 5017, Dunedin

Cover photograph: Hot-smoked Salmon Pâté page 8, Lamb Cutlets with Couscous Tabbouleh page 56, and Filo Tartlets with Lemon Cloud Filling page 78.

ISBN: 1-877168-90-4

TEXT: © Simon & Alison Holst

DESIGN: Dileva Design Ltd

PHOTOGRAPHY: © Hyndman except for pages 11, 33, 37, 39, 40, 43, 47, 49, 51, 54, 60, 62, 63 © New Holland

PHOTOGRAPHER: Lindsay Keats

PROPS: Chrissy Doring, Fiona Stewart

HOME ECONOMISTS: Simon & Alison Holst, Hilary Wilson-Hill

PRINTING: Tablet Colour Print

Important Information:

For best results, use a standard metric (250ml) measuring cup and metric measuring spoons when you use these recipes.
1 tablespoon holds 15ml.
1 teaspoon holds 5ml.

All the cup and spoon measures in the recipes are level, unless otherwise stated. Sets of measuring cups make it easier to measure ¼ and ½ cup quantities.

Larger amounts of butter are given by weight. Use pack markings as a guide. Small amounts of butter are measured using spoons (1 tablespoon of butter weighs about 15 grams).

Abbreviations used:

ml	millilitre
tsp	teaspoon
Tbsp	tablespoon
g	gram
°C	Celsius
cm	centimetre

Acknowledgements

We would like to thank the following:

Alison's Pantry for dried fruit, nuts, seeds and couscous.

Benniks Poultry Farm, Buller Road, Levin, for RSPCA approved barn-laid eggs.

Kapiti Cheeses Ltd for their prize-winning cheeses.

NZ Asparagus Council and The Tender Tips Company for fresh asparagus.

Pandoro for delicious fresh bread.

The New Zealand King Salmon Company Ltd for Regal salmon.

William Aitken Ltd for Lupi pasta, olive oils and balsamic vinegar.

Zespri International Ltd for Green and Gold kiwifruit.

Thanks to the following Wellington stores, **Freedom, Living & Giving, Moore Wilson's** and **Theme**, who provided the beautiful tableware used in the photographs.

This book combines the three bestselling books:

20 Minute Finger Food & Starters

20 Minute Quick & Easy Meals

20 Minute Desserts & After Dinner Treats

For more information about these (and other titles) visit:

www.hyndman.co.nz or www.holst.co.nz

For information about the kitchen utensils that Simon & Alison find invaluable, visit www.holst.co.nz or write to PO Box 17016, Wellington for a catalogue.

About this Book

We're all busy and there are many times and situations when we want to prepare a meal, or even just a snack, in a short time.

Whether you're rushing into the kitchen after work; returning home after ferrying children to after-school activities; finishing various home-based projects; or have just fed and bedded babies and toddlers, it is unlikely that you want to spend long in the kitchen. If you have asked friends to a meal, you'll want to spend as much time with them as possible, rather than slaving over a hot stove!

We hope to show that you can produce a remarkably wide range of good, interesting dishes in twenty minutes or less – without depending on processed, ready-to-eat foods or resorting to takeaways. (After all, 20 minutes is often less time than it takes to go out and buy takeaways.) Regardless of your cooking abilities, whether you need to make a few snacks to enjoy with friends over a drink, want a comfort-food style family meal, or are preparing a more elaborate three-course meal for guests, we hope you will find inspiration and solutions in this book.

In the past it was safe to assume that most households comprised two adults and two children; however, current statistics show that this is no longer the case. As a result, in some recipes we have given quantities for two or three adults and sometimes three or more. If you're using one of the recipes for two, but are cooking for a larger group, just multiply the ingredients accordingly, but bear in mind it may take a little longer to prepare and/or cook. (Before you halve recipes, stop to think whether it would be better to cook the larger quantity and refrigerate the part you don't want immediately. The "leftovers" can make nearly instant fast food.)

It is always hard to know exactly how long it takes someone else to prepare food. We know these recipes well, and know each dish can be made in 20 minutes or less (barring distractions by the phone, kids, etc.). When you make a recipe for the first time, it may take considerably longer than it will after you've made it a couple of times. Persevere and you'll be surprised just how quickly many of these recipes can be made.

While many of our desserts and treats can be made from start to finish and be ready to eat in 20 minutes, we have also included a few which are quick to prepare but need to be left (looking after themselves) to set in the refrigerator or to cook in the oven while you eat your main course.

This said, here are a few tips to help you speed up preparation:

■ Read your recipe and check what you already have before you go shopping.

■ Read the recipe from beginning to end, before you start.

■ Get out all the ingredients you need and arrange them in the order in which you will use them.

There are enough recipes in this book to get you through a whole month of meals with virtually no repetition. We hope you'll find these recipes useful and enjoy them as much as we do!

Happy cooking,

Simon Holst & Alison Holst

Finger Food & Starters

Whatever the occasion, whether it's pre-dinner snacks for a few friends or finger food for a crowd, we're sure you'll find something suitably tempting here. You will find these so good, you might even want to try several of them together to enjoy as an easy lunch or a tapas-style meal!

Herbed Chicken-liver Pâté

This easily made, smooth and creamy mixture is the most popular pâté we have ever made. Refrigerate leftovers for three to four days.

FOR ABOUT 400g, OR 2 CUPS:
100g butter
1½ tsp minced or very finely chopped garlic
400g chicken livers
2 Tbsp finely chopped fresh herbs such as thyme and oregano
2 Tbsp chopped fresh parsley
2 Tbsp Thai sweet chili sauce
¼ cup cream
2–4 Tbsp brandy or sherry (or a mixture of both)
freshly ground pepper
½ tsp salt

Melt the butter over moderate heat in a fairly large non-stick frypan. Stir in the garlic then add the chicken livers, straight from their pack.

Raise heat and cook chicken livers until no longer pink, turning frequently. For speed snip the large livers into much smaller pieces with scissors as they cook. Stir frequently adding the chopped herbs and chili sauce while livers cook. When cut surfaces are no longer red, after 5–6 minutes, the livers are cooked.

Add the cream, cook vigorously for about 30 seconds, then add the sherry and/or brandy and simmer for a minute longer. Turn off the heat, and add the pepper and salt.

Purée everything in the pan in a food processor while hot, then pour into a sieve. (A fine sieve produces the smoothest pâté.) For easiest sieving, bang the sieve on a fairly large bowl.

To cool the pâté quickly for immediate use, put the puréed mixture in a metal container and surround it with a mixture of ice blocks in cold water. Stir frequently for 1–2 minutes to remove the set mixture from the edges. When cold, transfer to serving bowl.

Let guests spread pâté on crostini, crackers, slices of French bread or other firm-textured, crusty bread. For contrasting colours and textures, serve carrot and celery sticks alongside if you like.

VARIATION: Serve the pâté before it cools and sets completely, as a dip for a selection of colourful, cold and crisp vegetables.

Hot Cream Dip ▼

This hot dip turns any crisp raw vegetables into something special. Its original name, Bagna Cauda, translates as 'Hot Bath.'

2 Tbsp butter
3 cloves garlic, finely chopped
6 flat anchovy fillets
1 cup cream
crisp, cold vegetables*

*Suitable vegetables include carrots, celery, radishes, cucumber, snow peas, cauliflower, capsicums of any colour, small crisp lettuce or Belgium endive leaves, zucchini, young tender beans, asparagus, button mushrooms, and cherry tomatoes. Choose a colourful selection and keep the pieces small enough to be easily managed.

Although it contains anchovies, this dip does not taste fishy. (There is no substitute for the anchovies in this recipe - if you don't like the idea of using them, just forget about making the dip!)

The fastest way to make this is to have one person make the dip while someone else prepares a large platter of vegetables to surround it.

Melt the butter, add the garlic and cook over a low heat for 1–2 minutes. Add the chopped anchovy fillets and cream, then bring to the boil and simmer for 4–5 minutes or until it thickens slightly, mashing the anchovies as they soften.

Serve the Bagna Cauda mixture hot or warm. Stand a candle under a heatproof container of dip to keep it hot and liquid, or put it in a microwaveable bowl and remove it every now and then to 'zap' it in the microwave oven at intervals. (The mixture will probably be too thick to dip when cool.) Surround the dipping bowl with a large selection of colourful chilled raw vegetables cut into dipping-sized pieces. Make sure you have plenty of cocktail napkins to prevent drips of dip falling on the carpet!

Hummus ▲

This is not a strongly flavoured, nor highly seasoned mixture, so is often eaten in larger quantities than many other dips or spreads.

300g can chickpeas
2–3 Tbsp lemon juice
1 large garlic clove, crushed
3–4 Tbsp tahini
3 Tbsp olive or other oil
liquid from can of chickpeas

NOTE: To make this dip without tahini:

Replace it with 1–2 teaspoons of Asian sesame oil.

OR add 2 rounded household tablespoons of peanut butter instead of tahini. Children often love this peanut butter version, especially with a couple of teaspoons of tomato sauce added for good measure!

OR if you have a spice grinder, grind about ¼ cup of lightly toasted sesame seeds and use them instead of tahini.

Drain the can of chickpeas, reserving the liquid. Put aside three or four chickpeas for garnish if you like.

Food process the rest of the canned chickpeas with the lemon juice, garlic and tahini until smooth, adding the oil in a thin stream. Thin it to the consistency of a spread or dip, with as much of the reserved chickpea liquid as you like.

Put the spread or dip in a small bowl, topped with the reserved chickpeas, and with a drizzle of olive oil or garlic-infused olive oil over it, if you like.

Serve with triangles of toasted pita bread, melba toast, crostini, crackers, or with a selection of raw vegetable crudités such as cauliflower florets, snow peas, carrots cut in strips or in diagonal slices, cucumber or celery strips.

NOTE: Tahini is a paste made from ground sesame seeds. Look for it in large supermarkets and stores that sell Middle Eastern foods. After opening, it may be kept in a cupboard for months, if not years. Stir the oil through the ground seeds before using it.

Smoked Fish Pâté ▸

Inexpensive whole sides (or fillets) of hot-smoked fish from the supermarket deli or fish department make interesting pâtés. Buy about twice the weight of fish that you need.

FOR ABOUT 1½–2 CUPS:
200g hot-smoked mackerel, kahawai or other fish (weighed after preparation)
125–250g cream cheese
2–3 gherkins, roughly chopped
1 Tbsp gherkin pickling liquid
1 Tbsp lemon juice
Tabasco or other chili sauce
1–2 tsp tomato paste (optional)
about ½ tsp salt

Remove and discard all the skin and bones from the fish sides or fillets. (Freeze extra fish for later use.) Purée the fish in a food processor with as much cream cheese as you like until thick and fairly smooth.

Add everything else and process until gherkins are finely chopped. Taste and add more salt if you like. If serving in a bowl, sprinkle with paprika for extra colour, if desired.

Serve on crusty bread, crostini, etc., or with raw vegetable crudités. Refrigerate leftover pâté for three or four days.

Hot-smoked Salmon Pâté ▸

This delicious dip has the attractive colour and appealing flavour of hot-smoked salmon. It may be used as a popular spread, too.

FOR ABOUT 1½ CUPS:
100–150g hot-smoked salmon
250g carton cream cheese
2 Tbsp lemon juice
1–2 Tbsp capers
1–2 Tbsp horseradish sauce (optional)
about 2 Tbsp chopped parsley, dill or chives
salt and pepper to taste

Put the salmon, cream cheese and lemon juice into a food processor and process until well mixed but not completely smooth. Add the capers, horseradish (if using) and the chopped herbs, and process, just enough to mix.

Season to taste then cover and refrigerate until required.

Serve spread on crusty bread, crackers, etc., or as a dip for vegetable crudités.

Crostini

Crostini are useful bases for many savouries, and good to serve with pâtés and dips.

Cut stale bread rolls or French bread crosswise or diagonally into 1cm slices. Brush with olive oil or spray with olive oil spray, and bake on baking paper or a non-stick liner at 150°C for 5-10 minutes until crisp and lightly browned. When cold, store in an airtight jar if you do not want to use them straight away.

For savoury crostini, instead of using plain olive oil, use a mixture of 4 parts of plain to 1 part of infused olive oil. Or add parmesan cheese, pesto, tapenade, ground cumin, mashed anchovies, etc. to the oil you are going to brush on the bread.

Blue Cheese "Starters" ▲

This smooth, well-flavoured mixture makes a basic "starter" which you can serve in different ways –

(a) Form it into a ball and roll in finely chopped walnuts. To serve, surround the ball with crackers.
(b) Shape it into a cylinder and roll in chopped walnuts – this looks neater for longer!
(c) Press it into a container and surround it with crackers. This keeps well for later use.
(d) Thin mixture with extra sherry, cream or yoghurt, to make a dip for vegetable crudités, potato crisps, crackers etc.

FOR CHEESE MIXTURE:
250g carton traditional cream cheese*
1 tsp onion pulp
1 tsp worcestershire sauce (optional)
1 tsp sherry
100g wedge (firm) blue vein cheese

FOR COATING:
½ cup finely chopped walnuts

FOR DIP:
sherry, cream or yoghurt

Spoon the cream cheese into a food processor or large mixing bowl in several blobs. Cut onion in half crosswise, and scrape the cut surface with the edge of a teaspoon to get onion pulp.

Add the worcestershire sauce (if using) and sherry. Break the wedge of blue cheese into the food processor bowl or coarsely grate it into the mixing bowl. Mix until blended.

If making a dip, thin to the consistency you want, as suggested above. Otherwise shape as suggested above. (If shaping a ball or cylinder, wrap the mixture in plastic film, shape, then chill it until firm before coating with the chopped nuts.)

Refrigerate leftovers (which are not covered with nuts or seeds) up to a week. (Coated mixtures are best eaten the day they are made.)

*Choose the firmest cream cheese available. Softer cream cheeses will be too soft to use for a ball or log, but will be fine in a lidded container or for a dip.

Guacamole ▶

Guacamole makes a colourful, easy and popular dip, topping and sauce!

1 ripe avocado
2 Tbsp lemon juice or 1 Tbsp lime juice
1 finely chopped spring onion
¼ tsp salt
Tabasco sauce to taste
chopped coriander leaves (optional)

Halve the avocado lengthways, then scoop the flesh into a bowl, making sure to scrape out the greenest flesh close to the shell. Mash with a fork, and add the remaining ingredients, using quantities to suit your taste. Use immediately.

Use straight away, as a dip for corn chips, as a topping for Mexican foods, crackers or crostini, and in other ways you like.

VARIATION: Replace all the seasonings above with about ¼ cup of Salsa Fresca and fold it through the mashed avocado.

◀ Simple Salsa Fresca

This basic tomato salsa is best the day it's made, but can be refrigerated for 2–3 days.

¼ red onion or 2 spring onions, roughly chopped
1 large clove garlic (optional)
1 tsp wine vinegar or 2 tsp lemon juice
½ tsp ground cumin
¼ tsp crumbled dried oregano
4 large fresh red tomatoes, roughly chopped
pinch of chili powder OR finely chopped fresh chili to taste
2–4 Tbsp coriander leaves
½–1 tsp each salt and sugar

Chop everything in a food processor (or chop everything by hand), put in a bowl and stir together. Use the smaller amounts of salt and sugar and process until mixed but still chunky. Taste and add more salt and sugar to balance the flavours as you like them. Leave to stand for 15 minutes before using, if possible.

Use as a dip with corn chips, spoon onto crostini, alone or with other toppings, or mix with mashed avocado to make an easy Guacamole.

Mexican Cheese & Tomato Dip ▾

This spicy and delicious hot dip is particularly welcome in cold weather. Buy twice as many corn chips as you think you will need, because they are likely to disappear really fast!

FOR 4–8 SERVINGS:
1 medium-sized onion, chopped
1 green pepper, chopped
1 Tbsp canola or other oil
1 tsp ground cumin
½ tsp ground coriander seeds
½ tsp smoked or plain paprika (optional)
1 Tbsp finely chopped jalapeno peppers (from a jar)
425g can chopped tomatoes
1 Tbsp flour
2 cups grated tasty cheese
¼ – ½ cup low-fat sour cream
coriander leaves or spring onions for garnish

Halve then peel the onion. Halve the pepper, and remove and discard all seeds and pith. Chop both into small (about 5mm) cubes. Cook these in the oil, without browning, for 3–4 minutes. Stir in the cumin, ground coriander and paprika (if using) and cook a minute longer.

Add the finely chopped jalapeno peppers, and 1–2 teaspoons of the liquid in the jar if you like an extra "tang" to this dip. Bring to the boil and add the contents of the can of tomatoes. (If you use a can of whole rather than chopped tomatoes, break them up.)

Toss the flour through the cheese, then stir into the hot tomato mixture until melted and smooth. Do not bring the mixture to the boil after the cheese has been added.

Serve hot, in a shallow dipping bowl, topped with sour cream and garnished with chopped coriander leaves or finely chopped spring onions. Serve surrounded by corn chips for dipping.

VARIATION: Make this dip without the green pepper if necessary. It is still very good! Replace ground coriander seeds with the same amount of dried oregano if you like.

NOTE: Look for pickled jalapeno peppers in jars in the Mexican food section of your supermarket.

Quesadillas ▶

Flour tortillas are a type of flat bread which may be turned into delicious, cheesy savouries, called quesadillas, in a very short time. Tortillas are thin, flexible and very versatile. (If you can't find "tortillas," look for other thin, flexible breads to use in the same ways.)

The tortillas may be crisped and their cheesy topping melted in a pan, under a grill or in the oven. Try them all three ways, to see which is fastest and easiest for you.

Flat Quesadillas

For flat (unfolded) quesadillas, brush outer edges (which will not be covered with cheese etc.) lightly with olive or canola oil.

Sprinkle the remaining surface with grated cheese. If you have time, chop several of the following into pea-sized pieces: red onions, olives, tomatoes, red or green peppers, brown flat mushrooms, avocado. Sprinkle these on evenly, add some canned Mexican bean mixtures and/or creamed corn and/or salsa if you like, then sprinkle a little more cheese on top.

Heat the tortilla flat in a heavy frypan, or grill it 5–8cm from the heat or bake it on an oven sheet at 180°C for 5–8 minutes. Cut in wedges with a heavy knife, eat as soon as the tortilla has browned and crisped, the cheese has melted, and other toppings are hot.

Folded Quesadillas

To make thin, cheese-filled crisp tortilla "sandwiches," lightly oil two flour tortillas. With the oiled side out, put grated cheese (and any extra flavourings suggested for flat quesadillas) between them. Cut into quarters before cooking, for easier turning and handling. Pan-cook, turning once, or grill, turning once, or bake (without turning) at 180°C for 5–8 minutes or until lightly browned and crisp.

Cut into smaller wedges soon after cooking, and eat while still warm and fairly crisp.

Eat just as they are, or as dippers, for guacamole and salsa.

VARIATION: You may find it easier to spread filling on only half of a tortilla which is to be cooked in a pan or under a grill. As soon as the tortilla has been heated enough to become flexible, flip the unfilled side over the filled side.

Chicken Quesadillas

Use cheese, a little salsa or chopped coriander leaves and chopped cooked chicken as a filling for folded quesadillas.

Spiced, Sugared Walnuts

These will keep for several weeks in an airtight jar.

2 cups walnut halves or large pieces
1 Tbsp egg white
½ cup icing sugar
1 Tbsp cornflour
½ tsp mixed spice
½ tsp salt

Turn oven to 125°C. Put walnuts in a bowl. Tip the measured lightly beaten but not frothy egg white onto the walnuts. Mix to coat thoroughly, using fingers. Sieve remaining ingredients into a shallow dish. Drop in the nuts and shake and turn them to coat. Arrange on non-stick liner or baking paper so they do not touch, and bake for 10–15 minutes until lightly browned and very crisp when cold.

Devilled Almonds

Heat these slowly so they don't brown before they heat through.

1 cup whole almonds
1 tsp sesame or other oil
1 Tbsp icing sugar
⅛–¼ tsp chili powder
1½ tsp each paprika and garlic salt
2 tsp Kikkoman soy sauce

Stir blanched or skin-on almonds and oil in a heavy frying pan to coat. Cook over low heat, stirring often, for 8–10 minutes, until a cut nut is very lightly browned. Mix the next four ingredients. Turn off heat, toss the hot nuts in the pan with soy sauce, then sift over the mixed seasonings and stir to coat. Cool. Store in an airtight container for 1–2 weeks.

Devilled Popcorn

Spicy popcorn is very popular but is too "hot" for young children.

Mix dry seasonings as for Devilled Almonds. Heat ¼–½ cup popping corn in 1–2 tablespoons of oil in a large, lidded pot until popped, drizzle in another 1–2 tablespoons of oil then sieve in the seasonings, while tossing with a fork. Eat immediately or store in an airtight jar, for up to two weeks. (Yield is 4–8 cups.)

Dukkah ▶

Dukkah is a highly flavoured mixture of nuts and spices. The crushed (but not powdered) mixture is made to suit individual preference, using what nuts and seeds are available and preferred.

FOR 2 CUPS:
½ cup sesame seeds
½ cup sunflower seeds
½ cup pumpkin seeds
1 cup blanched almonds
¼ cup cumin seeds
¼ cup coriander seeds
1 Tbsp (ground) paprika
1½ tsp rock salt
1½ tsp (ground) turmeric

olive oil for dipping
crusty bread chunks

Heat the oven to 180°C. Put the seeds and almonds in to roast, in separate foil dishes and/or pie plates, etc., in the order given. (We find that sesame and sunflower seeds take longer than the other nuts and seeds.) Watch carefully, checking them at least every 5 minutes, and take out each container when the seeds have darkened a little (but not a lot) and have an appetising aroma. (Most will take about 10 minutes.)

Leave the roasted nuts and seeds to cool, then grind with the paprika, salt and turmeric, in one or two batches in a food processor (using the pulse button), in a spice grinder, or with a pestle and mortar. The mixture should have some texture - it should not be ground to an oily powder.

Serve Dukkah in shallow bowls. Let your friends dip pieces of crusty bread into good quality olive oil, then into Dukkah.

Store extra in airtight containers in a cool place, away from direct light. It will gradually lose its flavour on long storage, but is still good after a couple of months.

NOTE: Try using Dukkah in other ways too. It is good sprinkled on an oiled chicken before roasting, and sprinkled over plainly cooked vegetables such as green beans.

▲ Marinated Feta & Olives

You can buy both marinated feta and different flavours of marinated olives but it is cheaper and far more satisfying to make your own – the results are impressive for very little effort.

FOR ABOUT 250g FETA (OR 200g OLIVES):
1–2 cloves garlic
1 small red chili
½ tsp black peppercorns
finely grated rind ½ lemon
few sprigs of thyme and rosemary, bruised
canola and olive oil, as required

Cut feta into bite-sized cubes or chunks (2cm cubes are good). Peel and halve or roughly chop the garlic clove/s and de-seed and slice the chili. Put a layer of feta cubes (or olives) in the bottom of your jar. (Don't pack them in too tightly, or the flavoured oil won't be able to reach all the surfaces.) Add a slice of garlic, a couple of slices of chili, a few peppercorns, a pinch of lemon rind and a sprig or two of the herbs. If you want the jar to look its best, poke some of the chili, garlic and herbs down the inside of the jar (between the cheese and the jar) so you can see it easily.

Repeat this layering until you have used all the cheese (or olives) and/or filled the jar. Add any remaining seasonings (unless you are going to start another jar), fill two thirds to three quarters of the jar with canola oil, then fill to the top with olive oil making sure all the cheese (or olives) is/are covered. (Canola oil is a light, flavourless oil that will carry the olive oil flavours. You can use olive oil only if you like, but it is much more expensive and sometimes turns cloudy when refrigerated.) Put the lid on the jar and invert a few times so the oil and flavourings are mixed.

Leave to stand for at least 15 minutes before serving.

NOTE: These make good gifts too, but they are not really suitable for long term storage – keep them in the fridge and use within 7–10 days.

VARIATION: Orange and Cardamom Olives: Use about 200g of mixed green and purplish (Kalamata) olives for interesting colour. Proceed as above, but using orange rind and 4-6 cardamom pods in place of the garlic, chili, lemon rind and herbs. Pour 1 Tbsp of orange juice over the olives before filling the jar with oil.

Antipasta Platters ▶

Antipasta platters or selections always seem popular in restaurants and cafés – it's fun to have a whole selection of different things delivered to your table! One of the nice things about an antipasta platter is that it requires only last minute assembly, (or you can arrange one in advance and refrigerate until required). A simple trip to the deli or supermarket* can provide all you require. You'll be amazed how appetising and substantial a collection of 6–10 different items from the list of suggestions below (2–3 from each category) can look. You don't need much of any one item, 50–100g is usually plenty.

VEGETABLES, FRUIT & NUTS:
Olives: plain, marinated or stuffed (use 1–3 different types on a platter)
Marinated artichoke hearts (marinated ones have much more flavour)
Char-grilled capsicums
Marinated mushrooms
Pickled onions
Pickled walnuts
Sun-dried (or semi-dried) tomatoes
Pickled vegetables (carrots, cauliflower, etc.)
Gherkins/dill pickles
Caper berries
Basil and/or tomato pesto
Tapenade
Raw vegetable crudités
Grapes
Sliced kiwifruit
Melon slices, balls or wedges
Dried fruit and/or nuts
Sliced avocado

CHEESES:
Cubed feta, marinated or plain
Camembert or brie styles
Aged cheddar
Blue cheese (mild or strong to taste)

MEATS:
Ham, shaved or cubed
Pastrami, shaved
Prosciutto, shaved
Peppered pork, shaved
Sliced salami (a couple of different types)
Sliced bierstick, chorizo or other pre-cooked sausage
Pâté, bought or homemade

SEAFOODS:
Thinly sliced smoked salmon
Flaked hot-smoked salmon or other fish
Smoked (or marinated) mussels
Smoked octopus
Roll-mops
Rolled anchovy fillets

Sliced bread/crackers etc. to accompany

*NOTE: Some of these items are available bottled and/or canned on supermarket shelves too – they are ideal for keeping in the pantry.

Asparagus Rolls ▲

Make these with lightly cooked fresh asparagus in season, and canned asparagus at other times.

Use fresh brown or white sandwich bread. Trim the fresh or canned asparagus stalks so they fit diagonally, corner to corner, across the bread. Allow 2 medium-thick stalks or 1 fat stalk for each slice of bread.

Boil trimmed stalks for about 4 minutes, until just tender and still bright green, then cool pot in cold water. OR put the cut lengths in an oven bag with 2 tablespoons of water. 16 medium-thick, cut stems usually weigh about 150g and microwave in 2 minutes on high (100%) power. Cool bag in cold water. Season with salt and pepper.

Cut crusts from sliced bread. Spread with softened butter flavoured with a little finely grated lemon rind. Place two medium stalks diagonally, top to tail, across bread. Roll up tightly, trimming off the inside corner for easier rolling. Roll finished asparagus rolls tightly in plastic film. When required, unroll plastic, cut rolls in half before serving.

Smoked Salmon with ▲ Horseradish

Cold-smoked salmon has a beautiful colour, delicious flavour and interesting texture. We always place it on top of savouries, where its colour will be most appreciated. Since it is very hard to cut thinly and evenly, we buy it already sliced, interleaved with plastic for easy handling.

TO MAKE HORSERADISH CREAM: Beat about 2 tablespoons of horseradish mixture (look for jars of grated horseradish flavoured with salt and sugar, since they have much more flavour than horseradish mayonnaise or dressing) with ½ cup of cream cheese until smooth. Taste and add more horseradish until it has the flavour you like.

Just before serving, spread it on the sliced crusty bread, then top with loose curls or folded strips of the cold-smoked salmon. Add a fresh herb garnish such as dill leaves, fresh fennel or chervil, and sprinkle with a few drops of lemon juice if you like.

Eggplant & Feta Rolls ▼

It's hard to give exact quantities for this since everything can be varied to suit your own tastes, mood etc. If you are making them as a starter, look for smaller eggplants (about 6cm thick), or cut wider strips from bigger eggplants in half lengthways once cooked.

FOR 10–12 ROLLS (5–6 SERVINGS):
2 small – medium (about 400g total) eggplants
3–4 Tbsp olive oil ('plain', basil or garlic infused)
1 medium red pepper*
1–2 Tbsp balsamic vinegar
100–150g feta
about 2 Tbsp chopped basil (or 10–12 basil leaves)
salt and pepper to taste

* If you are short of time, you can use bottled, char-grilled red pepper instead.

Cut the eggplants lengthways into thin (about 7mm) slices. Lightly brush both sides of each slice with oil. Place slices in a preheated contact grill (you may have to do this in several batches) and cook for 4–5 minutes on a high heat. OR arrange the slices on a non-stick sprayed baking sheet and place them under a preheated grill (5–7cm from the heat) and cook for about 3–4 minutes before turning and cooking a further 3 minutes. Set the cooked eggplant aside until cool enough to handle.

While the eggplant cools, prepare the remaining ingredients. If using a fresh pepper, cut the flesh from the core in flattish slices, brush these with any remaining oil and cook like the eggplant, then cut into 10–12 strips (you need the same number of strips as you have slices of eggplant). Cut the feta into the same number of fingers or slices too.

To assemble the rolls, lay a strip of eggplant on a board and brush lightly with balsamic vinegar. Lay a strip of red pepper and a piece of feta across one end, add a little chopped basil (or a basil leaf) then sprinkle with salt and pepper and roll up.

Arrange on a serving plate, drizzle with a little extra oil if desired and serve.

NOTE: If you want to serve Feta Rolls as a main course, use bigger eggplants cut a little thicker.

Bacon-wrapped Savouries

Who can resist warm little savouries made by wrapping thinly cut bacon slices around fresh oysters or scallops, plump prunes, firm little button mushrooms or inviting chunks of pineapple? Bake, grill or barbecue them until the bacon is crispy and aromatic, and the filling is heated through but not overcooked.

The bacon should be thinly cut, with the rind removed. It should be streaky but not too fatty. Cut the rind off each slice with a sharp knife or scissors, then stretch the bacon lengthwise. (Before you cut each slice into shorter lengths, wrap one of the items you are going to roll up in the bacon, allowing a little overlap, so you get the length right.)

Pour water over the small wooden or bamboo skewers which you will use to hold the bacon in place, and prepare the food which is to be rolled.

Drain oysters and scallops on paper towels. Squeeze a little lime or lemon juice and pepper over them.

Pour boiling water over pitted prunes and leave to stand for 2–3 minutes, then drain and pat dry. Leave as they are or stuff each with a drained canned water chestnut, a walnut half, or a few pinenuts.

Cut the stems from cleaned button mushrooms. Sprinkle with a few drops of lemon juice and worcestershire sauce, and your favourite infused olive oil. Wrap up a sprig of thyme with each mushroom if you like.

Cut fresh ripe pineapple into chunky pieces. Sprinkle with angostura bitters and Tabasco sauce if you like.

Roll food up in the bacon, secure with the skewers and refrigerate until required. Preheat the oven to 225°C with the rack just above the middle. Bake the savouries on low-sided containers lined with sprayed foil, baking paper or non-stick liners. Make sure that edges are raised slightly so that cooking juices do not drip on the bottom of the oven. Bake for 6–10 minutes, until the bacon is lightly browned and the fillings just heated through or cooked.

Serve straight after cooking, with small paper napkins.

VARIATIONS: Grill or barbecue the savouries close to the heat for 6–8 minutes, turning to brown both sides.

Spinach & Feta Packages

These very simple little packages are loosely based on Greek Spanakopita – they look great for a minimum of effort. They can be served hot, warm or cold so really are versatile.

FOR ABOUT 24-30 LITTLE PACKAGES:
1 Tbsp olive oil
1 medium onion, diced
¼ cup pine nuts (optional)
200-250g frozen spinach, thawed and drained
100-150g feta cheese, crumbled
¼ tsp dried basil
¼ tsp thyme
¼ tsp freshly grated nutmeg
¼–½ tsp salt
black pepper to taste
1 large egg
8–10 sheets filo pastry
about 2 Tbsp melted butter or olive oil

Turn the oven on to preheat to 200°C.

Heat the oil in a medium-sized frypan, add the onion and cook until softened. Stir in the pine nuts (if using) and continue to cook until these are golden brown.

While the onion cooks, squeeze as much liquid as you can from the thawed spinach. Place the spinach in a large bowl and add the crumbled cheese, then the seasonings and the onion-pine nut mixture. (The quantity of salt required will depend on the saltiness of the feta – vary it to taste.) Add the egg and stir until well mixed.

Lay one sheet of filo on a dry surface and brush it lightly with oil, cover with another sheet, then cut crossways into 6 strips (each should be about 8cm wide). Place about 1 tablespoon of the filling mixture close to one end of the first strip, then fold the corner up diagonally to cover the filling (so the bottom edge meets the side). Keep folding the filling (straight then diagonally) until you reach the end of the strip. Fold any extra pastry under the package, brush lightly with oil or melted butter and place on a baking tray. Repeat until all the filling is used.

Bake at 200°C for 8–10 minutes until golden brown and firm when pressed in the centre. Serve hot, warm or even cold.

Corn Fritters & Corn Cakes ▶

These little savouries are called cakes if they are cooked as small pancakes on a lightly oiled pan or barbecue plate, and fritters if they are fried in teaspoon lots.

FOR ABOUT 36 CORN CAKES:
1½ cups cooked corn kernels*
1 large egg
½ tsp salt
¼ cup milk
for cakes add 2 Tbsp extra milk and 1 Tbsp oil
1 cup self-raising flour

OPTIONAL ADDITIONS:
½ cup chopped roasted red peppers
½ cup chopped ham or cooked chicken
2 Tbsp chopped fresh herbs

chili, tomato or other sauce for dipping

*Use thawed frozen corn kernels cut from boiled or microwaved fresh corn cobs, or a 425g can of whole kernel corn.

Using a fork, beat the egg, salt and first measure of milk in a medium-sized mixing bowl. Add two extra tablespoons of milk and the oil if you are making cakes, but not if you are making fritters. Stir in the (drained) corn. Add any of the optional ingredients if desired.

Sprinkle the flour on top of the corn mixture. Using the fork or a flexible stirrer, stir the flour through everything else until you can see no pockets of dry flour. Do not mix until smooth, since over-mixing makes the cakes (or fritters) tough.

FOR CORN CAKES: Drop teaspoon lots on a preheated, oiled pan or griddle. If mixture does not spread, stir in a little extra milk. Turn when the cakes are lightly browned on the underside and are firm enough to turn over easily. Press the turned cakes down so that more of their surface touches the pan. The second side is cooked when the centre springs back when pressed. (If the cakes are too brown, or not brown enough when the bubbles burst, lower or raise the heat. Cook only one cake at a time until you get the heat right.) Top warm corn cakes with a wedge of avocado or Salsa Fresca (page 11) if you like.

FOR FRITTERS: Cook teaspoonfuls in preheated canola or other oil at least 1cm deep, turning as necessary, until the crust is evenly golden brown and the centre cooked. Serve on cocktail forks or small skewers, with chili, tomato or other sauce for dipping.

Chili Cheese Mini-Muffins ▶

These little muffins, made with strongly-flavoured cheese, fill the house with an irresistible aroma. For best flavour and texture serve them warm (but not hot).

FOR 24 MINI-MUFFINS:
2 cups (200g) grated tasty cheese
1½ cups self-raising flour
1 tsp garlic salt
2 Tbsp Thai sweet chili sauce
1 cup milk
1 large egg

Preheat the oven to 210°C. Use pre-grated cheese or grate it yourself. Measure the grated cheese, flour and garlic salt into a large bowl and toss gently with your fingertips to combine well.

Measure the Thai sweet chili sauce, milk and egg into a smaller bowl and beat with a fork until thoroughly combined. Pour the liquids into the dry ingredients all at once, then fold everything together, mixing no more than necessary to dampen the flour.

Using two dessertspoons, fill 24 mini-muffin pans which have been thoroughly sprayed with non-stick spray. Bake in the middle of the preheated oven for about 12 minutes, until the centres spring back when pressed and the muffins are golden brown. For easy removal from pans, leave muffins to stand 2–4 minutes before lifting out. (Some cheese may stick on the edges of the muffin tins. Remove it carefully.)

Serve warm muffins exactly as they come from the oven, on a folded serviette in a shallow basket or bowl.

OR cut a deep slash from the top, three quarters of the way to the bottom and insert a folded piece of cold-smoked salmon, salami, ham, cheese, a slice of a small tomato or a piece of roasted pepper, with a fresh herb leaf.

VARIATION: Add 2 tablespoons of chopped fresh herbs to the dry ingredients.

Smoked Salmon on Pesto Pancakes ▼

It takes only ten minutes to mix and cook these herby little pancakes – but you may find that they are eaten in even less time than this!

FOR 24–30 PANCAKES, 5cm ACROSS:
1 large egg
½ cup milk
1 tsp sugar
½ tsp salt
1 Tbsp basil or dill pesto
1 cup self-raising flour

crème fraîche, sour cream, cream cheese or mayonnaise
thinly sliced cucumber (optional)
about 100g thinly sliced smoked salmon
chives, dill leaves, basil or parsley

Heat a large, non-stick electric or regular frypan.

Beat the first five ingredients in a medium-sized bowl with a fork until everything is blended.

Add the carefully measured flour, then mix again with the fork just until the mixture is smooth. (Do not mix more than necessary.)

Drop the batter off the end of a dessertspoon onto the preheated pan, twisting the spoon as you drop the mixture, so each pancake is as round as possible. Turn each pancake as soon as you see the first few bubbles burst on the surface. Cook the second side until the centre springs back when pressed lightly. If the surface of the pancake is too brown, or not brown enough when the first bubbles break, alter the temperature of the pan. If pancakes are too thick, thin the mixture with a little extra milk. If not serving the pancakes straight away, overlap the cooked pancakes on several layers of paper towel and slip them, towel and all, into a plastic bag to stop them drying out.

To serve, spread a little of any of the creamy mixtures on the pancakes. Add a slice of cucumber if you like, then add a slightly "gathered" piece of thinly sliced salmon and a sprig of whatever herb you choose. Cover with plastic film until the savouries are passed round.

Whitebait Puffs ▲

Light, airy, with a delicate but recognisable flavour, these puffs make the most of a relatively small amount of Chinese whitebait – but you can use "the real McCoy" if you like!

FOR ABOUT 20 PUFFS:
150-200g (about 1 cup) frozen whitebait, thawed
2 large eggs, separated
½ tsp salt
1 Tbsp lemon juice
¼ cup self-raising flour
pepper to taste

Put a large, fairly heavy non-stick pan on to heat.

Run cold water through the whitebait in a sieve, then drain. Pick out any foreign bodies.

Break the eggs, putting the whites in a smaller bowl, and the yolks in a larger bowl. Add the salt to the whites and beat until they form peaks with tips which turn over at the top when the beater is lifted from them.

Mix the lemon juice, quarter of the beaten whites and the yolks, then stir in the flour. Stir in the drained whitebait, add remaining beaten whites, then fold everything together.

Drizzle a tablespoon of oil into the hot pan, tilt the pan so the bottom is covered, then drop dessertspoonfuls of mixture into the pan.

Cook until bubbles start to burst on the upper side of the puffs, then using a fork to stop the puffs sliding away, turn the puffs over with a thin, flexible blade. Cook the second side until lightly brown, then transfer to a plate in a warm oven until all the puffs are cooked. If the puffs are not light brown, adjust the heat when you cook the second batch.

Because the puffs are soft, place one or two (overlapping) on circles or ovals of French bread, or crustless rectangles of Vogels bread. Add dill or another herb and small lemon wedges for garnish, if you like. Serve as soon as possible after cooking.

Spicy Fish Cakes & Crab Cakes ▾

Made with or without the addition of crab meat, these little cakes are always very popular. Add a topping, if you like, or forget about the topping and serve them with a dip instead.

FOR 16–20 CAKES:
2 thick slices of bread
½ small red onion or 2 chopped spring onions
¼ cup roughly chopped coriander leaves, if available
1 large egg
about 2 tsp green curry paste
2 tsp fish sauce or ½ tsp salt
250g boneless, skinless fish fillets
100g surimi OR
   170g can crab meat OR 100g extra fish fillets

Break the bread into several pieces and put in a food processor with the roughly chopped onion (or spring onions) and coriander leaves. Process until the mixture is finely chopped. Add the egg and curry paste, using more or less according to the spiciness you want. Add the fish sauce or salt and process briefly to mix.

Chop the fish into 1cm cubes and add to the processor. If you are making crab cakes, add the chopped surimi or the canned crab and the liquid from the can as well. Pulse in bursts, until fish is chopped in small pieces but is not puréed. (Under-processed fish will tend to fall apart in fingers when picked up, while over-processed fish turns tough and rubbery. Experiment, cooking a small amount of the mixture as soon as you think it is sufficiently mixed.)

Heat about a tablespoon of canola or grapeseed oil in a large, non-stick pan, form the fish mixture into bite-sized cakes, and cook over moderate heat for about 2 minutes per side, until lightly browned.

Serve soon after cooking, or reheat until warm in a microwave oven. If you like, top the hot or reheated cakes with a little sour cream or crème fraîche and a small amount of salmon caviar or lumpfish caviar. Garnish with dill or coriander leaves.

NOTE: We prefer the flavour of crab cakes made with surimi to that of crab cakes made with canned crab.

Crispy Wontons ▲

Wonton skins are fun to fill and shape. Look for wonton skins in Asian food stores or large supermarkets.

FOR 40–50 WONTONS:
40–50 wonton skins
400g minced pork or chicken
1 Tbsp sherry or lemon juice
2 Tbsp Kikkoman soy sauce
1 Tbsp cornflour
1 tsp sesame oil
2–3 spring onions
2 Tbsp finely chopped coriander leaves (optional)

canola oil or other oil for frying
chili, tomato, or sweet and sour sauce for dipping

Thaw (wrapped) wonton skins if necessary. Put the minced pork or chicken in a bowl or food processor. Add the next four ingredients and mix with a fork or process to blend. Chop the spring onions and coriander very finely and mix them through the meat.

Tip the completed filling onto a board, divide it into four equal parts, then divide each part into 10–12 small blobs.

Before you shape the wontons put the oil on to heat. You need oil 2cm deep in a wok or medium-sized pot. It is hot enough when an unfilled skin turns golden-brown in one minute.

Take 4 wonton skins at a time and put a blob of filling in the middle of each. Dampen the skin surrounding the meat with a little water, then fold one edge over the filling, until it meets the other side, forming a triangle. Press the wonton skin together around the meat. Next, bend the folded corners towards each other, pinching them firmly together. (It doesn't really matter how you fold the wonton as long as the filling is completely enclosed.)

Lower the shaped wontons carefully into the hot oil, cooking two to four at a time. Turn them over if necessary. Cool cooked wontons on paper towels for a minute. Serve warm, with a sauce such as sweet chili sauce for dipping.

Rice Paper Rolls ▶

These rice paper rolls are simple and delicious. For maximum ease just pick up half a cooked chicken at the supermarket as we have here.

FOR 12–20 ROLLS*:
1 clove garlic, chopped
1–2 tsp grated ginger
2 Tbsp each water, Kikkoman soy sauce and sherry
1 Tbsp brown sugar
½ tsp five spice powder
½ tsp cornflour

200–250g cooked chicken meat, shredded
12–20 rice paper wrappers
½ medium lettuce, finely shredded
1 medium carrot, grated
2–3 Tbsp chopped coriander or mint (or a mixture)
¼ cup chopped peanuts (optional)
12–20 small spring onions or garlic chives (optional)

*We use wrappers that are about 15cm across to make starter-sized rolls, but you can use bigger or smaller ones if desired.

Stir the first eight ingredients together in a small pot or microwave bowl, and heat to boiling (microwave for about 1 minute) until the sauce thickens and turns clear.

Place the shredded chicken in a small bowl, add the thickened mixture and toss to mix. (Store in fridge if preparing in advance.)

To make the rolls, soak the wrappers (3–4 at a time) in warm water until soft and white (about 20–40 seconds depending on the wrappers). Lift a wrapper out of the water, let it drain for a few seconds then lie it flat on a board. Place a little shredded chicken, some lettuce, carrot, a pinch of coriander and/or mint and a few chopped peanuts (if using) in the middle of the wrapper. Fold in the bottom and side edges to make an envelope shape, lie a spring onion or chive on top (if using), then roll up to make a little parcel.

Arrange completed rolls on a plate or platter, covering with cling film or a clean damp cloth if preparing in advance. Serve as is, or accompanied with a Vietnamese-style dipping sauce (combine the juice of 1 lime or lemon, ¼ cup each water and fish sauce, 1 Tbsp caster sugar, 2 cloves finely chopped garlic and 1 finely chopped small red chili, leave to stand for 5 minutes then serve).

Soy-glazed Chicken Nibbles ▼

In a microwave oven, these tasty chicken pieces can be cooked in a very short time.

FOR 4–6 SERVINGS:
500g chicken "nibbles"
2 Tbsp dark soy sauce or
 ¼ cup Kikkoman soy sauce
2 Tbsp sherry
2 Tbsp brown sugar
about 1 tsp finely chopped or grated garlic
about 1 tsp finely grated root ginger
2 tsp sesame oil
1 tsp cornflour
2 Tbsp toasted sesame seeds

Put the chicken nibbles (individual chicken wing joints) in an oven bag then add all the remaining ingredients except the sesame seeds. Knead the bag gently but thoroughly to mix everything well. Fasten the neck of the bag with a rubber band, leaving a finger-sized opening so that the bag does not blow up like a balloon during cooking. Leave the pieces to stand in the marinade for at least 5 minutes before cooking.

To cook, lie the bag of chicken pieces and marinade flat on the floor of the microwave oven so the chicken pieces are in one layer. Check that the opening of the bag is not obstructed. Microwave on full power for 10 minutes, then flip bag over, and leave it to stand for 2 minutes. Pierce the thickest piece to check that it is cooked – if pink juice runs out, cook chicken for longer, in 1 minute bursts, until the juice from another pierced piece is clear.

Remove the cooked chicken pieces from the bag, sprinkle them with toasted sesame seeds immediately, then leave to stand for about 2 minutes, until the pieces darken and appear glazed. Pass small paper napkins around with the chicken, and eat with fingers while warm.

Oriental Meatballs ▲

We sautéed, microwaved and baked these tasty little meatballs. Baked meatballs were easiest, sautéed meatballs looked best, but those microwaved were fine too.

FOR 48 SMALL MEATBALLS:
1 medium onion, chopped
2 cloves garlic
2–3 spring onions, sliced
¼ cup chopped coriander leaves (if available)
450–500g minced beef or pork
¼ cup fine dry breadcrumbs
1 egg
1 Tbsp cornflour
1 Tbsp each Kikkoman soy sauce and sesame oil
½ tsp salt
½ tsp sugar
2 Tbsp Thai sweet chili sauce

Put the first four ingredients in a food processor and chop finely. Add everything else except the chili sauce, then process in bursts until you get a smooth mixture which forms balls that don't break.

Divide mixture into eighths on a board, then divide each eighth into six even pieces. Roll each piece into a small ball and cook balls soon after shaping.

TO BAKE: Place the shaped balls in a large, shallow baking dish, on a non-stick liner. Bake at 200°C for about 12 minutes, or until a ball, cut in half, is no longer pink in the middle (brush with the chili sauce after 8 minutes).

TO SAUTÉ: Cook in a preheated, large, non-stick pan in a dribble of oil. Jiggle the pan while the balls brown, to keep them nice and round, then drizzle them with Thai chili sauce. Cover pan and cook for 2–3 minutes longer, until a cut ball is no longer pink in the middle.

TO MICROWAVE: Replace the Kikkoman soy sauce with dark soy sauce. Place half the balls in a circle around the edge of a microwave turntable. Brush with Thai chili sauce mixed with a teaspoon of dark soy sauce. Microwave uncovered, at full power, for 3–4 minutes. Stand for 1 minute then halve a ball to see if it is cooked through. If not, cook 1 more minute then test again. Cook remaining mixture in the same way.

Serve on toothpicks, with your favourite dipping sauce, and with paper napkins to stop drips.

Chicken & Mushroom Dumplings ▾

Surprise and delight your friends with these delicious little packages!

FOR ABOUT 30 DUMPLINGS / DIM SUM:
3 dried (shitake) mushrooms
2 Tbsp dry sherry
1 Tbsp Kikkoman soy sauce
2 cloves garlic
1 Tbsp finely chopped or grated ginger
1 egg
300g chicken mince
1 spring onion, thinly sliced
2 Tbsp chopped coriander leaf
about 30 sui mai or wonton wrappers (thawed if frozen)

soy and sweet chili sauce for dipping

Finely chop the dried mushrooms (from Asian food stores or some supermarkets), place in a small container, cover with sherry and soy sauce and microwave on high (100%) power for 1 minute (or bring to the boil on the stove top). Leave to stand while you prepare everything else.

Finely chop the garlic and place in a medium-sized bowl. Add the finely grated ginger, then the egg, and whisk lightly. Tip in the chicken mince, the sliced spring onion, chopped coriander leaf and the soaked mushrooms, then mix until everything is evenly combined.

Round sui mai wrappers (about 8cm across) from the frozen foods section of Asian food stores are ideal, but wonton wrappers (which can be found in some supermarkets) with the four corners trimmed off so they are roughly octagonal, also work well.

Place about a heaped teaspoon of the filling mixture in the centre of a wrapper, then gather up the edges and squeeze gently to form a "money-bag-shaped" parcel that is slightly open at the neck. Repeat until all filling is used.

Place the parcels in non-stick sprayed steamer baskets, 1cm apart. Cover and steam over rapidly boiling water for 7-10 minutes, until pastry is soft and filling is firm.

Serve immediately, with little bowls of soy and sweet chili sauce for dipping.

Thai-style Spring Rolls ▲

These mini-spring rolls are delicious and remarkably simple to prepare as the filling requires no precooking, just a little assembly.

FOR 20–30 LITTLE ROLLS:
½ cup lightly packed rice vermicelli*
1 cup very finely sliced cabbage
1 medium carrot, grated
2–3 Tbsp roasted peanuts, chopped
1 Tbsp each oyster sauce, fish sauce and Thai sweet chili sauce
1 Tbsp chopped coriander (optional)
1 tsp sesame oil
¼ tsp each salt and sugar

20–30 (10cm square) wonton or spring roll wrappers
1 tsp cornflour mixed with 2 Tbsp water

soy and sweet chili sauce for dipping
canola or other oil for frying

Soak the noodles in warm water for five minutes while you prepare and measure the remaining filling ingredients into a medium-sized bowl. Drain the noodles well, then add them to the other filling ingredients and toss to mix.

Lie a wrapper on a board with a corner pointing towards you (like a diamond), then spread about 2 teaspoons of the filling in a line across the wrapper just below half way. (Don't be too generous with the filling, or you won't be able to fit it in!)

Fold the left and righthand corners towards the middle so the ends of the filling are covered, then, working from the corner near you, roll the wrapper up so the filling is completely enclosed. Seal the end by moistening the flap with a little of the cornflour-water mixture. Repeat this process until you have used all the filling mixture, or all the wrappers.

Heat the oil in a wok or small frypan and fry the rolls, five or six at a time, turning occasionally until golden brown. Drain the cooked spring rolls on paper towels and serve warm, accompanied with bowls of soy and sweet chili sauce for dipping.

*Very fine, clear-looking noodles (like threads of glass – they are sometimes called glass noodles) available from stores specialising in Asian foods, or from larger supermarkets.

Quick & Easy Mains

Whether you want traditional family-friendly comfort food or more trendy "café-style" favourites for entertaining friends, you'll find a good selection here – and each of these mains can be prepared without spending hours in the kitchen.

◁ Ten Minute Salmon & Couscous Salad

Made with your favourite salad vegetables, this all-in-one salad is just the thing when you don't want to cook at the end of a hot summer day.

FOR 2–3 SERVINGS:
1 can (100–200g) salmon
1½ cups liquid (see method)
½ tsp minced chili (optional)
¾ cup couscous
2 spring onions, chopped
1–2 tender celery stalks, sliced
2–3 cups torn or roughly chopped lettuce leaves
about 1 cup chopped cucumber
about 1 cup coarsely chopped red tomatoes
chopped fresh coriander leaves, basil, dill, etc.
juice of 1 lemon
2–3 Tbsp olive (or other) oil
salt and pepper to taste

Use whatever sized can of salmon suits you. Drain the liquid from the canned salmon into a measuring jug and make up to 1½ cups with chicken stock (or 1 teaspoon instant chicken stock and water). Stir in the chili if using it, then bring mixture to the boil in a microwave oven or pot.

Tip the couscous into a large, shallow, heatproof bowl. Pour the heated liquid over it, cover the bowl with a plate and leave to stand for 6 minutes while you prepare everything else.

Prepare all the vegetables, keeping the cubed tomatoes separate. (Add other suitable vegetables or use replacements if desired.) Chop up or tear the herbs.

When the couscous has soaked up all the liquid, break the drained salmon into chunks and mix it lightly through the warm couscous with about half the lemon juice and oil. Taste and season if necessary, then add the prepared vegetables (except tomatoes) and herbs and fork everything together. Drizzle with remaining lemon juice and oil, top with the cubed tomatoes and serve straight away, piled into shallow bowls. Eat just as it is, or with crusty bread rolls.

VARIATIONS: Add cooked prawns, and/or mussels, surimi, or chopped hardboiled eggs.

Replace lemon juice and oil with salad dressing.

Replace couscous and stock with cooked rice or pasta.

Chicken Salad, Vietnamese-style ▲

This interesting salad makes a good, quick, warm weather meal when served with crusty bread or plain rice. Its strongly flavoured dressing is fat-free.

FOR 3–4 MAIN SERVINGS:

DRESSING:
2 Tbsp fish sauce
2 Tbsp lime juice or 3 Tbsp lemon juice
2 Tbsp caster sugar
½–1 tsp minced chili
1 Tbsp each chopped coriander leaves, mint and basil

SALAD:
350–500g roast or smoked cooked chicken
½ medium-sized cabbage
3 spring onions
15cm length of cucumber
1 carrot
½ cup chopped roasted (or honey roasted) peanuts
about 1 cup torn basil, mint, coriander and/or rau ram leaves

First make the dressing. Put the first three ingredients in a jar, adding chili to taste, then add the finely chopped herbs, using whichever are available. Shake to dissolve the sugar, then taste and add extra sugar if you like, especially if you have used lime juice. Put the dressing aside.

To prepare the salad, slice the warm or cold chicken into thin strips. Slice the cabbage thinly, as you would for coleslaw. Diagonally slice most of the leaves and all of the white part of the spring onions. Halve the cucumber lengthwise, and scoop out and discard the seeds using a teaspoon. Then cut the rest into matchsticks, 5cm long. Food process the carrot into long strips or cut it into matchsticks like the cucumber. Chop the peanuts (honey roasted peanuts are particularly good) and tear whichever herbs are available into bite-sized bits. (Rau ram is Vietnamese mint and tastes like peppery coriander leaves.)

If you are serving the salad immediately, combine all ingredients and the dressing in a large shallow bowl and mix gently but thoroughly. (Clean fingers do a good job here!) If preparing ahead, refrigerate individual salad ingredients in plastic bags, adding a little cold water to the cabbage, spring onions, carrot and herb leaves to keep them crisp until required.

Pile salads attractively on individual plates. Serve with plainly cooked rice (see page 44) or noodles in separate bowls, or with crusty bread rolls.

Pasta Niçoise ▾

The flavours of this salad are based on the classic Niçoise salad, but we've given it a twist by replacing potatoes with pasta and using a mayonnaise-based dressing.

FOR 2–3 SERVINGS:
250g small pasta shells
2 eggs
150g fresh green beans
3–4 medium-sized ripe tomatoes
12–16 black olives
1–2 Tbsp capers
½ cup mayonnaise
2 Tbsp lemon juice
2 Tbsp olive oil
½ tsp salt
black pepper
210g can tuna (in oil or brine)
¼ cup chopped fresh parsley

Put pasta on to cook in plenty of boiling water and the eggs on to hard-boil. (Prick the rounded end of the shells to prevent bursting and add the eggs to the pasta water, if you want.)

Top and tail the green beans, then boil or steam until tender. Cool in cold water, then cut into 4–5cm lengths.

Cube the ripe tomatoes and place these in a bowl. Add the cooked beans and the olives and capers. Toss these together, then add the mayonnaise, lemon juice, oil, salt and pepper. Mix again until well combined.

Open and drain the tuna, then add to the vegetable mixture, flaking but not mashing it.

Drain the cooked pasta (removing the eggs), then add the tuna mixture and the chopped parsley. Stir gently to combine. Transfer to a serving bowl (or bowls) and garnish with the quartered or roughly chopped hard-boiled eggs.

Serve warm or chilled, either alone or with crusty bread.

Chunky Corn & Ham Chowder ▲

A big bowl of this thick, creamy soup, packed with corn, other vegetables and ham, makes a satisfying meal on a cold day.

FOR 4 LARGE SERVINGS:
1 Tbsp oil
½–1 tsp minced or finely chopped garlic
1 large onion
1 medium-sized carrot
2 cups hot water
1 leek or 2 tender celery stalks (optional)
2 medium-large potatoes (about 300g)
2–3 tsp instant chicken or bacon stock
50g butter
¼ cup flour
2 cups milk
2 tsp basil pesto (optional)
440g can cream-style corn
100–200g chunky ham pieces
chopped parsley and chives

In a large pot over moderate heat, heat the oil and garlic while you chop the halved, peeled onion into 7mm cubes. Stir the prepared onion into the oil and keep cooking the mixture while you chop the scrubbed carrot into slightly smaller cubes (the carrot will not cook in time if cut into large cubes). Add the hot water, then the prepared carrot. While this mixture simmers, add the thinly sliced celery and the scrubbed potatoes, cut into 7mm cubes. Add the instant stock, cover the pot and leave the vegetables to finish cooking while you make the sauce.

Melt the butter in a medium-large pot. Stir in the flour and heat until it bubbles, without letting it brown. Add the milk, half a cup at a time, stirring constantly and bringing to the boil before the next addition. When it boils after the last milk is added, take it off the heat and stir in the pesto (if you have it) and the corn.

As soon as the potato and carrot are tender, tip the sauce and the finely chopped ham and parsley or chives into the large pot with them, stir to mix thoroughly, and heat through, without actually letting the mixture boil. Serve in large bowls with (warmed) crusty bread or rolls.

VARIATIONS: Leave out the ham, but brown 2–4 chopped bacon rashers in the oil before adding the garlic and chopped onion. To save time, replace the onion, carrot and celery with 4 cups frozen vegetables.

Pasta & Bean Soup ▼

This version of a 'classic' Italian soup is not only delicious, it is very quick to prepare when you use canned beans. Served with crusty bread, it makes a really substantial meal.

FOR 4–6 SERVINGS:
3 Tbsp olive oil
1 clove of garlic, peeled and chopped
1 medium onion, quartered and sliced
50–100g cubed ham or chopped bacon (optional)
2 small dried chilies, crushed (or ½ tsp chili powder)
2 bay leaves
¼ tsp dried thyme
400g can whole tomatoes in juice
425g can red kidney beans
440g can four bean mix
4 cups chicken or vegetable stock
(or 4 cups water plus 3–4 tsp instant stock powder)

1 cup (100g) short pasta (macaroni, spirals, rigatoni, etc.)
½–1 tsp salt
black pepper to taste
chopped, fresh parsley or basil pesto and/or parmesan to serve

Heat the oil in a large pot. Add the garlic and onion (plus ham or bacon, if using) and cook, without browning, until the onion is soft and clear. Stir in the crushed chilies, bay leaves and thyme. Cook for one minute longer.

Add the canned tomatoes, beans and the stock. Heat until boiling, then add the pasta. Allow to boil gently until the pasta is cooked (usually 10–12 minutes), then add salt and black pepper to taste.

Serve topped with some chopped fresh parsley or basil (or a little pesto) and some freshly shaved or grated parmesan.

Seafood Laksa ▶

We both love Malaysian Laksas from Asian food halls and market stalls. This recipe gives a great Laksa 'fix' at home.

FOR 3–4 SERVINGS:
2 Tbsp curry powder
2–3 Tbsp blanched almonds or cashew nuts
2–3cm piece fresh ginger, peeled
2 cloves garlic, peeled
2–3 Tbsp chopped fresh lemon grass, or finely chopped rind of 1 lime
1–2 tsp Thai red curry paste (optional)
2 Tbsp each light soy sauce and water
2 Tbsp canola oil
400ml can coconut cream
3 cups water
3 tsp instant chicken stock
500g fresh egg noodles*
400–500g firm fish fillets, cut in 2–3cm cubes
1 medium-large carrot, cut into matchsticks
100g spinach leaves, Asian greens or green beans
100–200g cooked prawns (optional)
100–200g bean sprouts
chopped fresh coriander leaves and/or spring onion to garnish

Combine the first eight ingredients in a blender or food processor (or use a mortar and pestle) and process to make a smooth paste. (The Thai curry paste is not absolutely necessary, but it adds to the 'depth' of flavour.)

Heat the oil in a large pot, then add the paste and cook, stirring continuously for 1 minute. Add the coconut cream, water and instant stock. Bring the soup to the boil and add the noodles, fish, carrot and green vegetables and simmer for 2–3 minutes until the cubes of fish are just cooked through. During this time divide the prawns and bean sprouts between the serving bowls.

Ladle the soup into the bowls (you may need tongs to lift the noodles), dividing the fish etc. evenly between each. Garnish with a few extra bean sprouts, some chopped coriander leaves and/or sliced spring onion and serve immediately.

*Fresh egg noodles may be replaced with rice sticks (from larger supermarkets and Asian food stores), which keep almost indefinitely in the pantry. Simply soak 250g of thick rice sticks in boiling water for 5 minutes, then divide them between the bowls with the prawns and sprouts rather than simmering them in the soup.

Fish Chowder for all Seasons ▼

Fish chowder makes an excellent meal at any time of the year. This version is light enough to serve during summer but is also warm and comforting on a cold winter's evening.

FOR 3–4 SERVINGS:
1 Tbsp olive oil
25g butter
1 medium onion, diced
100g bacon, cut into 1cm squares
2 sticks celery, thinly sliced
2 medium potatoes, cut into 1cm cubes
1 medium carrot, finely diced
2½ cups milk
½ tsp garlic salt
500g fish fillets, cubed
1 Tbsp chopped fresh dill (optional)
1 Tbsp cornflour
salt and pepper to taste
chopped fresh dill or parsley to garnish

Heat oil and butter together in a large pot, then add the diced onion and cook until soft. Add the bacon, celery, potatoes and carrot and cook, stirring frequently to prevent browning, for about 5 minutes.

Add 2 cups of milk and the garlic salt and simmer for 10 minutes or until the potato is tender, then add the cubed fish and dill. Mix remaining milk with the cornflour and add to the pot. Bring to the boil, then reduce heat and simmer for 5 minutes.

Season to taste with salt and pepper, then ladle chowder into large bowls, garnish with chopped dill or parsley and serve with crusty garlic bread (page 46).

Fish Battercakes ▲

This easy recipe is very popular with children who like crisp, crunchy coatings. It makes fish go further and works well with soft texture fish (red or blue cod, moki or hoki).

FOR 4–5 SERVINGS:
canola or other flavourless oil for frying
400–500g boneless, skinless fish fillets (see above)
1 egg
½ cup milk
1 tsp salt
½–1 tsp curry powder
½–1 tsp paprika (optional)
1 cup self-raising flour

Heat a large, preferably non-stick frypan containing oil 5mm deep. If the pan is thermostatically controlled, set it to 190°C (or to the second highest number).

Cut the fish into 1cm cubes, removing any bones and skin. Put aside until the batter is ready.

In a fairly large bowl, mix together the egg and milk. Mix together the remaining ingredients (using amounts to suit), then sprinkle the mixture over the egg and milk. Stir until partly mixed but still rather lumpy, then fold the cubed fish through the batter, stopping while batter still looks rough rather than smooth. (Over-mixing makes battercakes tough.) There should be just enough batter to hold the fish together and partly coat it.

Drop spoonfuls into the hot oil, helping mixture off with another spoon. Cook over moderate heat. Turn each battercake with tongs (or a fish-slice) when the bottom is golden. Cook the second side in the same way. The centre is cooked when a pointed knife comes out without uncooked batter on it. Do not cook any longer than necessary.

Serve with lemon wedges or tartare or tomato sauce, quick potato wedges (see page 60) or bread rolls, and small (or chopped) tomatoes and/or a green salad.

VARIATIONS: For Oyster Battercakes, add 6 chopped oysters to fish. For Mussel Battercakes, replace cubed fish with 25–40 steamed, chopped mussels (see page 46).

Fish Veracruz ▾

This easy fish dish has a delicious Mexican flavour and it can easily be cooked from start to finish while the rice to serve it on cooks in the microwave. (See page 44.)

FOR 3–4 SERVINGS:
2 Tbsp olive oil
1 medium onion, sliced
2–3 cloves garlic, crushed, peeled and chopped
2 dried red chilies,* deseeded and sliced
1 green pepper, deseeded, quartered and sliced
2 bay leaves
1 tsp cumin
½ tsp oregano
400g can whole tomatoes in juice
500g firm-fleshed fish fillets, cubed (snapper, monkfish, warehou, etc.)
1–2 Tbsp chopped fresh coriander leaves
1 Tbsp lime (or lemon) juice
about ½ tsp salt

Heat the oil in a large frypan. Add the onion and garlic and cook until the onion softens, then add the chilies, green pepper and the bay leaves.

Continue to cook, stirring occasionally, until the onion is translucent and the green pepper is soft. Add the cumin and oregano. Drain the tomatoes, reserving the juice, then crush the whole tomatoes and add them to the pan with about half the juice.

Carefully stir in the cubed fish and simmer gently for about 5 minutes, stirring once or twice to turn the fish. (Add the remaining tomato liquid if the mixture begins to look dry.) Remove from the heat as soon as the largest cubes of fish are just cooked and stir in the coriander leaves, lime (or lemon) juice and salt to taste.

Serve immediately over plainly cooked rice (see page 44). A crisp green salad (see page 49) and cold beer make ideal accompaniments.

*The dried chilies we use for this are 5–7.5cm long (from Asian food stores) and are hot but not as 'fiery hot' as their tiny and more widely available cousins.

Sweet Chili Salmon on Sesame Noodles ▶

Like most fish, salmon cooks very quickly, so this tasty and elegant meal for two really can be prepared quickly.

FOR 2 SERVINGS:
about 300g salmon fillets
¼ cup sweet chili sauce
3–4 Tbsp chopped coriander leaves
1 Tbsp lime or lemon juice
1 Tbsp Kikkoman soy sauce
2 tsp sesame oil
200g noodles (Asian egg noodles, soba noodles, vermicelli etc.)
1 medium carrot, julienned or grated
10–15cm telegraph cucumber, deseeded and julienned or grated
about 100g daikon*, julienned or grated (optional)
1 Tbsp canola oil
1 Tbsp sesame oil
1 Tbsp Kikkoman soy sauce
1 tsp grated ginger
1 Tbsp toasted sesame seeds

*Daikon is a large, white radish available in supermarkets. It may be refrigerated and used over 1–2 weeks.

Cut the salmon into serving-sized pieces, then place in a plastic bag and add the next five ingredients. Massage the bag so the salmon is coated, then set aside. Turn the grill on to preheat, placing a grill tray 7–10cm below the element.

Meanwhile, bring a large pot of lightly salted water to the boil. Add the noodles and cook until tender. (The time will vary according to the type of noodle you use.) While the noodles cook, prepare the vegetables. When the noodles are cooked, drain them well and rinse briefly with cold water. Return the noodles to the cooking pot, add the remaining ingredients and toss to mix.

Arrange the marinated salmon pieces, skin-side down, on a double layer of foil, and (carefully) place this on the heated grill tray. (This helps the skin-side cook.) Grill the salmon 7–10cm from the heat for 3–5 minutes, depending on thickness.

Place the cooked salmon on a nest of the warm sesame-noodle mixture and serve immediately.

Fish Tikka Masala ▶

This creamy fish curry tastes so good that it's hard to believe it's so simple to prepare! We don't often use fenugreek seeds, but they really do give this dish a distinctive flavour.

FOR 4 SERVINGS:
1½ cups long grain rice* (see cooking instructions)
500–600g fairly firm fish (tarakihi, monkfish, warehou, etc.)
¼ cup plain unsweetened yoghurt
1 Tbsp each honey and lemon juice
1 clove garlic, crushed, peeled and chopped
1 tsp each cumin, coriander and fenugreek seeds
400g can whole tomatoes in juice
¾ cup cream
2 Tbsp grated ginger
1 Tbsp each tomato paste and honey
1 tsp salt
½ tsp chili powder
1 tsp garam masala
2–3 Tbsp chopped fresh coriander leaves

*Use basmati or fragrant rice if you have them.

Cut the fish into cubes or chunks 2–3cm thick, then place in a plastic bag with the yoghurt, first measure of honey, lemon juice and garlic. Massage the bag so the fish is evenly coated with the marinade mixture. Set fish aside while you turn the grill on to heat and make the sauce.

To make the sauce, place the whole spices (seeds) in a large, dry pan and heat until they smell toasted and fragrant. Transfer to a blender (or mortar and pestle) and grind, then add the next six ingredients and process again until smooth. Pour the mixture into the pan and heat to boiling, then reduce the heat and leave to simmer gently while you cook the fish.

Arrange fish on a lightly oiled, foil-covered tray, then grill about 5cm from heat for 5 minutes. Add garam masala and coriander leaves to sauce, stir to mix, then gently add the grilled fish and simmer for 2–3 minutes longer.

Fluff the cooked rice with fork. Top with fish mixture. Serve with Indian bread.

TO COOK THE RICE: TO MICROWAVE: Measure the rice into a large microwave bowl, add 3 cups of boiling water and ½ teaspoon salt (optional), then cover tightly and microwave for 15–17 minutes on medium (50%) power. **TO BOIL:** Bring 10 cups of water, plus 2 teaspoons salt, to a rapid boil. Sprinkle in the rice and boil uncovered for 10–12 minutes or until rice is tender, then drain well.

Mussels in Spiced Tomato Sauce ▶

This is a really satisfying (and inexpensive) meal for mussel lovers! Serve it on fresh or quick-cooking pasta, rice, or split, toasted rolls as a complete meal.

FOR 2–3 SERVINGS:
1 cup boiling water
½ cup white wine or chicken stock
¼–½ cup roughly chopped mixed fresh herbs or 1 tsp each
    dried oregano and thyme
1–1.25kg fresh, live mussels
2 Tbsp canola or other oil
1 medium-sized onion
½–1 tsp chopped garlic
½ tsp each ground cumin and curry powder
2 Tbsp flour
1 cup strained mussel-cooking liquid
400g can whole or chopped tomatoes in juice
2–3 Tbsp cream or sour cream
chopped fresh herbs to garnish (optional)

To cook the mussels, put water with wine or stock and herbs into a large pot and bring to the boil while you wash the mussels. Discard any which stay open when tapped and put the rest into the boiling liquid. Cover and cook for 2 minutes, then shake pot, but leave on high heat. Lift mussels, as they open, onto a shallow tray or plate, after tipping their liquid back into the pot. When all are cooked, strain. Put aside 1 cup of cooking liquid.

Meanwhile, cook pasta or rice (see page 44) or toast split bread rolls.

Make the sauce. While mussels cook, heat a large non-stick pan. Add the oil, chopped onion and garlic, and brown lightly over medium heat. Stir the cumin, curry powder and flour into the onion mixture, then add the reserved mussel liquid, tomatoes and juice. Simmer for 3-4 minutes, stirring at intervals, while you attend to the cooked mussels. Add the cream to the thickened sauce and season to taste.

Leave the cooked mussels in their shells, or remove one shell from each mussel, or take mussels out of their shells completely.

Serve mussels, sauce and extra herbs on the drained pasta, rice, or toasted rolls, sprinkled with the extra chopped herbs or parsley if you like.

Garlic Bread ▼

For four slices of easy garlic bread, mix 2 tablespoons of olive oil (or melted butter) with a finely chopped clove of fresh garlic. Lightly brush both sides of thick, diagonally cut (this makes the pieces of bread longer) slices of French, or other, bread with the garlic mixture, then grill on a plain or ridged hot plate or under direct heat, turning once, until both sides are golden brown.

Pasta with Salami & Broccoli ▲

This meal is best when made just before it is needed. For maximum flavour and texture, combine the sauce, cooked pasta and broccoli at the last minute.

FOR 2–3 SERVINGS:
150–200g fettuccine or large spirals
about 200g fresh broccoli
3 Tbsp butter
2 garlic cloves, finely chopped
½ cup chicken stock or 1 tsp instant chicken stock dissolved in
   ½ cup water
½ cup cream or sour cream
1 tsp Dijon mustard
⅛ tsp chili powder
about 50g salami
3–4 spring onions, finely chopped
¼ cup grated parmesan cheese

Put the pasta on to cook in plenty of lightly salted, boiling water. Use the larger or smaller amount, depending on appetites!

While pasta cooks, cut the florets from the broccoli stalks. (If you want to cook the stalks as well, peel them first, so they will be just as tender as the florets.) Cook the prepared broccoli in a covered pan over fairly high heat, in 1 tablespoon of water and 1 tablespoon of the butter, for 2–3 minutes, until just tender and still bright green.

Meanwhile, melt the rest of the butter in a medium-sized frypan. Add the garlic and cook briefly, then add the chicken stock, cream (or sour cream), mustard and chili powder and bring to the boil, stirring all the time. Remove from the heat and put aside.

Cut the salami into matchsticks. Thinly slice the spring onions. Stir these into the hot, prepared sauce. Add the grated parmesan cheese and stir.

Check to see if the pasta is cooked by tasting a piece. When cooked, drain it well and stir in the hot, drained broccoli (including any of its remaining, buttery cooking liquid) and the hot sauce. Serve straight away, alone, or with a salad.

For a really simple tomato salad, cube halved tomatoes and sprinkle with a little salt, pepper and sugar.

Penne with Bacon & Mushroom Sauce ▼

This delicious sauce can easily be prepared in the time it takes the pasta to cook. Simply add a salad and maybe some bread for a really easy meal.

FOR 2–3 SERVINGS:
250g penne or other pasta
150g bacon
2 Tbsp olive oil
1 medium onion, diced
150g button mushrooms, sliced
½ tsp dried sage
½ tsp dried thyme
½ tsp salt
black pepper
¼ cup vegetable stock or white wine
½ cup cream
fresh thyme, parsley and/or parmesan to garnish

Put on a large pot of water for the pasta. Prepare the sauce while waiting for the water to boil and the pasta to cook.

Cut the bacon crossways into 1cm strips. Heat the oil in a large pan, then cook the bacon until it is brown and turning crispy. Remove the bacon from the pan and set it aside to drain on paper towels. Pour excess fat from the pan, leaving about 2 tablespoons, and add the diced onion. Sauté until the onion is soft and clear then add the sliced mushrooms and cook, stirring frequently until these soften.

Add the seasonings and the stock or wine. Simmer over a moderate heat for 2 minutes, then add the cream. Increase the heat so the sauce is boiling vigorously and cook for another two minutes, stirring frequently. Allow the sauce to reduce down and thicken a little.

Drain the pasta as soon as it is cooked, then return it to the pot and add the sauce. Stir to mix thoroughly. Leave to stand for one to two minutes, then serve topped with a little fresh thyme, parsley and/or some grated parmesan.

For the easiest of salads to serve alongside, just buy a few handfuls (or a tub) of mesclun (mixed baby salad greens) from the supermarket. Store in the fridge until required, then immediately before serving simply drizzle with a little lemon juice and some good olive oil. Add a grind of black pepper and perhaps a sprinkling of salt or a few shavings of parmesan, then toss and serve.

Fettuccine with Ham & Peas ▸

This sauce isn't exactly low in fat, but it is simple, delicious and quick to prepare. These mitigating factors help make it a good meal for a special occasion.

FOR 3–4 SERVINGS:
1 tsp olive oil
50g butter
200g ham
1 Tbsp flour
300ml cream
¼ cup white wine, water or milk
1 cup frozen peas
1 Tbsp basil pesto
½ tsp salt
black pepper to taste
400g fresh or dried fettuccine

Start by putting on a large pot of water for the pasta. While the water heats, prepare the sauce.

Heat a medium-large pan to make the sauce, then add the oil followed by the butter. While the butter heats, slice the ham (fairly thinly), then cut the slices crossways to give narrow strips or matchsticks.

Sauté the ham in the butter, stirring frequently, until it has turned golden brown. Stir in the flour and cook for a minute longer. Pour in the cream and wine (or water or milk) and allow the mixture to come to the boil before adding the peas and seasonings.

Reduce the heat to very low (or turn off the element but don't remove the pan) and leave to simmer gently while you cook the pasta. Drain the cooked pasta and toss with a little olive oil (or additional butter) before gently stirring the sauce through it.

Serve immediately, topped with a generous grind of pepper and/or some chopped fresh herbs and grated parmesan.

For an interesting salad to serve on the side, cut 4–5 medium-sized tomatoes into 1.5–2cm cubes. Place them in a bowl and add a pinch of salt and sugar, 1–2 teaspoons balsamic vinegar and 1–2 tablespoons olive oil. Stir gently to mix, then sprinkle with black pepper and a little chopped basil, if available.

Beef Stroganoff ▸

This quickly-cooked luxury meal is great for special occasions. It is especially good when made with smoked paprika, which gives a lovely rich, smoky flavour.

FOR 2–3 SERVINGS:
200g fresh fettuccine or 150g dried ribbon-shaped pasta
1 large onion
2 Tbsp each butter and olive or canola oil
200–250g large flat mushrooms
¼ cup white wine
½ cup beef or chicken stock or 1 tsp instant stock and ½ cup hot water
1 tsp tomato paste (optional)
2 Tbsp brandy or sherry (optional)
200–250g fillet steak cut in pencil-sized strips
1 Tbsp flour
½ tsp paprika
2 Tbsp sour cream

Get everything out before you start to cook. Heat a large pot of boiling, salted water for the pasta. Put dried pasta in to cook straight away. Cook fresh pasta later.

Halve onion lengthways, then slice it crosswise into pencil-width strips. Cook in a large non-stick pan, using half the butter and oil to brown lightly. Slice mushrooms into strips of similar width. Raise the heat, add the mushrooms and cook for 1–2 minutes. (The mushrooms will look dry.) Add the wine, stock, tomato paste and brandy or sherry (or extra stock) and cover and cook for 4–5 minutes on high heat, stirring occasionally.

Meanwhile, slice the steak into pencil-thick strips, heat a smaller non-stick pan to cook it in, and drain the cooked pasta. Toss the steak in the flour and paprika, heat the remaining butter and oil, and briefly cook the steak over high heat, turning it often, until it has browned. Stir steak and half the sour cream into the mushroom mixture and heat through. Thin the sauce if necessary.

Spoon meat and mushroom mixture on the pasta, top with remaining sour cream, and sprinkle with more paprika.

Serve with salad greens that have been drizzled with a little olive oil and lemon juice just before serving.

VARIATIONS: If the steak pan has a good non-stick finish, use only half the remaining oil and butter to cook it. Cook 200g whole, young green beans with the pasta.

Grilled Chicken on Lemony Orzo

Orzo (or risone) is little rice-shaped pasta – it's been around forever but is fashionable at the moment. It can be used a bit like rice but it cooks faster, so it's ideal when time is short.

FOR 2–3 SERVINGS:
300–400g chicken tenders (tenderloins) or other boneless, skinless chicken, cut into strips
1 lemon, zested and juiced
2 cloves garlic, crushed, peeled and chopped
2 Tbsp chopped parsley
½ tsp minced red chili
2 Tbsp olive oil
1 medium onion, diced
1 cup orzo
2½ cups boiling water
2 tsp instant chicken stock
2 zucchini, diced
½ red pepper, diced
10–20 Kalamata olives (optional)
50–100g feta cheese, crumbled
1 Tbsp olive oil (optional)

Place the chicken tenders, or strips, in a plastic bag with half of the lemon zest, 2 tablespoons lemon juice, the garlic, parsley, minced chili and 1 tablespoon of olive oil. Massage bag so the chicken is coated with the marinade, then set aside. Turn the grill on to preheat.

Heat the second tablespoon of olive oil in a large, lidded pan. Add the onion and sauté until soft. Stir in the orzo and remaining lemon zest, then add the boiling water and instant stock. Cover and simmer for 8–10 minutes, or until just tender through. (If the mixture begins to look too dry, add an extra ½ cup water.)

While the orzo cooks, arrange the chicken on a non-stick sprayed tray. Place under the grill 7–10cm from the heat and cook for 4–5 minutes before turning and cooking for a further 3–4 minutes or until cooked through. (Test by cutting a piece in half through the thickest part — if there is no pink left it is cooked.) Remove from the heat and set aside to stand as soon as cooked.

Stir the vegetables, olives (if you like them) and any remaining lemon juice into the orzo mixture. Cover and simmer for 2–3 minutes longer, then remove from the heat and stir the crumbled feta (and optional olive oil) through the mixture.

Pile the orzo onto serving plates and top with the chicken strips. Serve immediately, accompanied with a simple green (see page 49) or tomato salad (see page 50) if desired.

Stir-fried Chicken & Mushrooms ▾

Chicken and mushrooms always work well together and this tasty stir-fry is no exception. Prepare everything before you start cooking, as once you start it all happens very fast!

FOR 2–3 SERVINGS:
250–350g boneless, skinless chicken thighs or breasts
1 Tbsp dark soy sauce
1 large clove garlic, crushed, peeled and chopped
2–3cm ginger, finely chopped
250g button mushrooms, halved or quartered
5–6 spring onions, white and green parts cut diagonally into 3cm pieces
3 Tbsp canola oil
1 tsp cornflour
2 Tbsp sherry or rice wine
1 Tbsp dark soy sauce
1 tsp sesame oil
½ tsp sugar
2–3 Tbsp coriander leaves (optional)

If you are going to serve the chicken on rice, cook 1 cup long grain rice according to the instructions on page 44. If you are going to use noodles, cook according to packet instructions, drain, then return them to the cooking pot and toss with a little oil.

Cut the chicken (across the grain) into slices 5–7mm thick. Place in bowl or plastic bag and add the first measure of soy sauce, garlic and ginger then stir to mix well. Set aside while you measure and prepare the mushrooms and onions.

When everything is ready, heat 2 tablespoons of the oil in a wok or pan over a high heat. Add the chicken and stir-fry for 2–3 minutes or until chicken is no longer pink. Remove the chicken from the wok or pan and set aside.

Heat the remaining oil and add the mushrooms and spring onions. Stir-fry until the mushrooms have just softened, 2–3 minutes. Mix the cornflour, sherry, second measure of soy sauce, sesame oil and sugar together well and add to the wok/pan. Toss together until the sauce thickens. (Add 1–2 tablespoons of water if you want more sauce.)

Stir in the coriander leaves (if using), then spoon the chicken and mushroom mixture over the rice or noodles and serve immediately.

Green Chicken Curry ▼

For something so easy to make, this Thai-style green curry really is delicious! Kaffir lime leaves give a really distinctive flavour, if you can find them.

FOR 3–4 SERVINGS:

2 Tbsp canola oil
1–2 Tbsp Thai green curry paste
1 medium onion, sliced
1 medium potato, cut into 1cm cubes
3–4 kaffir lime leaves*, cut into strips about 1cm wide (optional)
300–400g boneless skinless chicken thighs or breasts, cubed
1 cup coconut cream
2–3 zucchini, sliced
½ cup peas or green beans, fresh or frozen
150–200g can bamboo shoots, drained (optional)
¼–½ cup water (if required)
2 Tbsp fish sauce
1 tsp sugar
salt to taste
handful fresh basil leaves (optional)

* Look for these in Asian food stores. Sometimes available fresh, otherwise frozen or dried.

Since this curry cooks very quickly, start by putting the rice on to cook. You can make plain 'steamed' rice (page 44) or try it with coconut rice (see below).

Heat the oil in a frypan or wok. Stir in the curry paste and cook for about a minute, then add the onion, potato and lime leaves (if you have them). Stir-fry for 1–2 minutes longer.

Add the chicken and stir, then carefully pour in the coconut cream and simmer for 5 minutes, stirring occasionally.

Add the vegetables and bamboo shoots (if using) and thin the sauce with ¼–½ cup water, if required. Simmer until chicken is cooked through and vegetables are just tender – about 10 minutes in all. Add the fish sauce and sugar. Taste and add salt, if required. Stir in the basil leaves (if using).

Serve over rice and garnish with a few extra basil leaves.

COCONUT RICE:
Place 1 cup of fragrant Thai or basmati rice in a microwave jug or bowl. Add ½–¾ cup coconut cream, ½ teaspoon salt, 1 teaspoon sugar and 1½ cups boiling water, then cover and microwave at medium (50%) power for 15–17 minutes.

Lamb (or Chicken) Satay ▲

Satay kebabs with peanut sauce are always a popular starter, but when served on rice and accompanied with a salad they also make a great meal.

FOR 2–3 SERVINGS:
2 cloves garlic, peeled and chopped
½ tsp each ground cumin and coriander
¼ tsp chili powder
2 Tbsp each lemon juice and peanut butter
1 Tbsp canola oil
400g cubed lamb (or boneless, skinless chicken thighs or breasts)
8–10 bamboo skewers

SATAY SAUCE:
1 clove garlic, peeled
1–2 tsp grated ginger
¼ cup crunchy peanut butter
½ cup boiling water
1 Tbsp light soy sauce
2 tsp sesame oil
1 tsp brown sugar
½ tsp minced red chili or chili powder
1–2 Tbsp chopped coriander leaves (optional)
salt to taste

Measure the first seven ingredients into a plastic bag and massage to mix. Add the cubed lamb (or chicken) and massage the bag so the meat is covered with the marinade.

Cover the skewers with hot water and set them aside to soak while you prepare the rice and preheat the grill.

Put plain (page 44) or coconut rice (page 54) on to cook.

Thread the meat onto the soaked skewers, then place them 5–10cm below the preheated grill and cook for 6–8 minutes, turning once.

While kebabs cook, prepare the sauce. Place all the ingredients, except coriander leaves and salt, in a blender or food processor and blend or process until well combined. Transfer into a small pot (or microwave bowl) and heat until the sauce has thickened, then add coriander and salt to taste.

Spoon the cooked rice onto serving plates, then arrange the kebabs over the rice. Pour the sauce over the kebabs, or serve it separately on the side.

For an interesting salad accompaniment, try this wilted cucumber salad: halve 10–15cm of telegraph cucumber lengthways. Scoop out and discard the seeds, then slice thinly. Soak for 10 minutes in ½ teaspoon salt dissolved in ½ cup of cold water. Drain, then toss with 1 chopped spring onion and 1 tablespoon wine vinegar.

Lamb Cutlets with Couscous Tabbouleh ▶

This is a good meal for a hot summer evening. When you buy cutlets, make sure that they are "chined" with the knobbly bit at the top of the rib bone removed.

FOR 2-3 SERVINGS:
6–9 (chined) lamb cutlets

MARINADE:
1 tsp chopped or minced garlic
2 tsp lemon juice or 1 tsp balsamic vinegar
¼ tsp crumbled, dried oregano
1½ Tbsp olive oil

COUSCOUS TABBOULEH:
¾ cup couscous
½ tsp salt
½ tsp minced chili
1¼ cups boiling water
2 Tbsp lemon juice
2 spring onions, chopped
2 cups cubed red tomatoes
about ¼ cup chopped mint
¼–½ cup chopped parsley
2 Tbsp olive oil

Put the cutlets between two sheets of plastic (or a large, folded plastic bag) and beat them with a rolling pin until the eye of the meat is twice the size that it was originally.

Stir the marinade ingredients together on a shallow plate that will hold the flattened cutlets, then turn the cutlets in the mixture. Cover with plastic and leave to stand while you prepare the tabbouleh. Put a large non-stick frypan on to heat.

To make the couscous tabbouleh, put the couscous, salt and chili in a medium-sized bowl. Stir in the boiling water and lemon juice and leave to stand, without stirring, for about 6 minutes. Meanwhile, finely slice the spring onions, including most of the leaves. Cut the tomatoes into 1cm cubes, and finely chop the mint and parsley.

Put the cutlets in the pan and cook about 1½ minutes per side.

While lamb cooks, fork the spring onions, tomatoes, herbs and olive oil through the tabbouleh and pile on plates. Serve cutlets (or kebabs) leaning against the tabbouleh as soon as lamb is cooked. Serve alone or with crusty bread.

Spicy Pork Fillet on Kumara Mash ▼

This recipe is seasoned for adults' taste. We often cook whole beans on top of the kumara and add a few flat mushrooms to the pan with the pork. Delicious!

FOR 2 SERVINGS:

SPICY PORK FILLET:
about 250g pork fillet, in one piece
½ tsp each minced garlic, ginger and chili
2 tsp Kikkoman soy sauce
2 tsp sesame oil
1 Tbsp sherry
1 Tbsp apricot jam

KUMARA MASH:
1 medium onion, finely chopped
2 Tbsp olive oil
½ tsp each minced garlic and ginger
350g yellow or orange kumara
¾ cup water
salt to taste

OPTIONAL VEGETABLES:
about 150g whole green beans
2–4 flat mushrooms

Put fillet on plastic. Score both sides with shallow, diagonal cuts, in a diamond pattern. Fold plastic over fillet and bang with a rolling pin until half its original thickness. (During cooking, fillet will contract again.) Put fillet and everything but the apricot jam in a plastic bag and leave to stand.

Prepare kumara mash. Heat onion in a pot with the oil, garlic and ginger while you peel and halve the kumara lengthways. Cut it in 5mm slices and boil in the salted water (lid on) for about 7 minutes, until soft. Add whole beans to pot after kumara has cooked for about 2 minutes. Water should almost have evaporated when kumara is cooked. Put beans on warm plates in oven, and mash or pureé kumara, adding salt to taste.

While kumara cooks, heat a large, non-stick pan with a dribble of oil. Take fillet from marinade and cook on high heat for about 5 minutes per side. Add mushrooms to the pan after 5 minutes. Put cooked mushrooms on plates in oven after 3–4 minutes. Add the pork marinade and the apricot jam to the pan, turning fillet to glaze evenly as it cooks. Leave to stand for a minute, then cut in half diagonally. If still pink in the middle, either microwave it on high (100%) power for 1 minute or slice the whole fillet and return it to the pan for about a minute, so the slices finish cooking in the glaze.

Pile mash on plates, top with pork, and put beans and mushrooms alongside. Drizzle thinned glaze over pork.

Easy Tostadas ▲

Our ever-popular "Easy Tostadas" are a great casual meal. Make them from tortillas, fried flat and topped with beef and beans, shredded cheese and lettuce, etc. (see below).

FOR ABOUT 4 SERVINGS:
1 Tbsp oil
1 large onion, preferably red
1 tsp chopped garlic
½–1 tsp minced chili
350–500g minced beef
2 tsp ground cumin
1 tsp each oregano, salt and sugar
400g can kidney beans
¼ cup tomato paste
about ½ cup water
8–12 corn or flour tortillas
oil for frying

TOPPINGS:
shredded cheese
shredded lettuce
chopped tomatoes
chopped peppers
sliced avocado
sliced spring onions
chopped coriander leaves

Heat the oil in a fairly large non-stick pan. Add the finely chopped onion, the garlic and the chili, and cook on moderate heat for 1–2 minutes. Raise the heat and add the minced beef, breaking it up and browning it. Stir in the cumin, oregano, salt and sugar, the beans and their liquid and the tomato paste and water. Cover and simmer for about 10 minutes. Add extra liquid if mixture is too thick to spread easily, or cook uncovered if it seems very liquid.

While the beef and bean mixture cooks, fry the tortillas* one at a time, in hot oil about 5mm deep. Press the tortillas into the oil with tongs, turning when the first side is golden brown. Drain on paper towels.

Prepare the listed toppings, putting each in a separate bowl, so diners can help themselves at the table, or let them collect a tostada, some beef and bean mixture, and a selection of toppings from a side table. Sprinkle avocado with lemon juice to stop it browning or mash it with lemon juice.

Put out a bowl of salsa (commercially made or prepared from the recipe on page 61), or Guacamole (page 11). Home-made salsa (without avocado) may be made ahead and refrigerated for about two days.

Eat with your fingers or with a fork, depending on tortilla size and the occasion!

*Look for freshly made N.Z. tortillas and other flat breads at your supermarket.

Home-made Hamburgers ▼

Home-made burgers make a great quick and easy meal. It sounds clichéd but hot off your own stove (or barbecue) they really are quite different to anything you can buy.

FOR 4 'QUARTER-POUND' BURGERS:
500g minced beef
1 cup (2–3 slices bread) soft breadcrumbs
1 large egg
1 tsp garlic salt
black pepper to taste

TOPPINGS:
sliced tomato
lettuce leaves or coleslaw
sliced cheese
fried egg
red, yellow and green peppers (raw or roasted)
sautéed mushrooms
sliced gherkins or dill pickles
thinly sliced red onion
sliced avocado
sliced beetroot
watercress or other fresh herbs
chili beans and sour cream

Place all the ingredients in a large bowl, then mix thoroughly. (Clean hands work best for this.) Divide the mixture into 4 balls then flatten these into roundish patties – it doesn't matter if they're not perfectly round.

Grill or barbecue the patties about 20cm from the heat, turning when browned (or brown the patties on both sides in a hot, lightly oiled frypan). Lower heat and cook until the centre is firm when pressed.

What really makes burgers are the extras, but it's better not to go too far. Serve in lightly toasted plain or sesame buns with three or four of the toppings given opposite.

Of course, no burger is complete without tomato sauce and/or mustard.

For an ideal accompaniment why not make your own potato wedges? Heat the oven to 220°C. Quarter scrubbed, unpeeled potatoes lengthways (allow 1 to 1½ medium potatoes per person), then cut each quarter (lengthways) into 3 wedges. Place wedges in a plastic bag and toss with 1-2 teaspoons oil per potato. Arrange wedges in a single layer on a non-stick sprayed (or Teflon or baking-paper lined) tray. Sprinkle lightly with garlic salt, paprika and pepper, then bake for 12-15 minutes or until golden brown.

Corn Cakes with Salsa ▲

Served with the salsa given below, these delicious corn cakes (or fritters) make a quick and tasty meal.

FOR 3–4 SERVINGS:
SALSA:
2 firm, ripe, tomatoes, deseeded and diced
1 medium avocado, peeled and diced
½ red onion, diced
2 Tbsp chopped fresh coriander leaves
1–2 Tbsp each lemon juice and sweet chili sauce
salt and pepper to taste

CAKES OR FRITTERS:
1 cup self-raising flour
2 large eggs
½ cup beer (or soda water, milk, etc.)
2 Tbsp Thai sweet chili sauce
1 tsp each cumin and paprika
½ tsp salt
1½–2 cups fresh, frozen or (well drained) canned corn kernels
2 spring onions, finely sliced
2–3 Tbsp chopped coriander leaves
1 medium red (or green) pepper, deseeded and diced
oil to fry (see method)

To make the salsa, toss the tomatoes, avocado, onion and coriander together in a small bowl. Add enough lemon juice and chili sauce to moisten thoroughly, then stir. Season to taste with salt and pepper, then leave to stand while you cook the cakes or fritters.

To make corn cakes (or fritters), measure the flour into a medium-sized bowl. Add the eggs, beer (or other liquid), chili sauce, spices and salt, then stir together to make a smooth batter.

Add the corn, spring onions, coriander leaves and pepper to the batter and stir just enough to combine.

Heat the oil in a large non-stick pan. For corn cakes use just 1–2 tablespoons; for 'traditional' fritters, use oil 5–10mm deep. Carefully drop spoonfuls of batter into the pan, cooking batches of fritters for 3–5 minutes per side until golden brown, or cooking cakes until they are lightly browned on both sides and firm when pressed in the centre.

Drain cooked fritters on several layers of paper towels. Keep cooked fritters or cakes warm in the oven until all the mixture is cooked, then stack them on plates and serve immediately, topped with the salsa.

NOTE: If using fresh corn, stand the 'naked' cob upright on its stem end. Cut kernels off the cob using a sharp (or serrated) knife.

Chickpea & Spinach Curry ▼

This is a great vegetarian meal. It makes an easy and delicious meal on its own, but is even more interesting when served with an array of Indian condiments.

FOR 4 LARGE SERVINGS:

2 Tbsp canola oil
1 large onion, diced
2 cloves garlic, crushed, peeled and chopped
1 Tbsp finely chopped ginger
2–3 medium (250g) potatoes, cut into 1cm cubes
2–3 tsp curry powder (mild or hot to taste)
½–1 tsp cumin seeds (optional)
2–3 bay leaves
250g package frozen spinach, thawed
400g can whole tomatoes in juice
310g can chickpeas, drained
¼–½ cup water, if required
2 tsp garam masala
salt and pepper to taste
2 Tbsp chopped fresh coriander leaves

Heat the oil in a large pan. Add the onion, garlic and ginger and stir-fry until the onion has softened and is turning clear. Add the cubed potatoes, curry powder, cumin seeds (if using) and bay leaves. Cook for 1–2 minutes, then add the spinach with its liquid and the tomatoes in juice. Crush and break up the tomatoes, then stir in the drained chickpeas.

Simmer the mixture gently for 15 minutes, or until the potato cubes are tender, adding a little water if the mixture begins to look too dry. When the potatoes are cooked, add the garam masala, season to taste with salt and pepper and add the chopped coriander leaves.

For a simple meal serve the curry in bowls as it is. Alternatively, serve with plain rice (see page 44) or coconut rice (see page 54), naan bread or poppadums and assorted chutneys and relishes.

Curried Cauliflower & Eggs ▲

Non-cauliflower lovers (like Simon) usually find this delicious!
Even if cauliflower is not your favourite vegetable, give it a
try – it really is good.

FOR 3–4 LARGE SERVINGS:
4 large eggs
1 Tbsp canola oil
1 medium onion, quartered and sliced
2 medium-small potatoes (200g total) cut into 1cm cubes
2 cloves garlic, crushed, peeled and chopped
1 Tbsp finely grated ginger
1 Tbsp curry powder
2 cardamom pods, crushed (optional)
4–5 whole cloves (optional)
400g can whole tomatoes in juice
¾ cup coconut cream
250g cauliflower, cut into florets
1 tsp garam masala
½ cup frozen peas (optional)
1–2 Tbsp chopped fresh coriander leaves
½ tsp salt

Put the eggs in a small pot and cover with hot water, then
bring to the boil and simmer for 12 minutes. (Making a
small hole in the blunt end of each egg will help prevent
them cracking or splitting.)

While the eggs cook, heat the oil in a large pan, then add
the onion, potatoes, garlic and ginger. Cook, stirring
occasionally, for 5 minutes, then add the curry powder and
the whole spices (if using). Continue to cook, stirring
frequently, for 1 minute longer, then add the tomatoes in
their juice. Break up the tomatoes with a spoon, stir, then
cover the mixture and simmer gently until the potatoes are
tender, about 5 minutes. Drain the cooked eggs, cover with
cold water to cool, then peel and cut into quarters and set
them aside.

Stir the coconut cream, cauliflower florets and garam masala
into the curry mixture. Simmer uncovered for another five
minutes, or until the cauliflower is tender. Mix in the peas (if
using), coriander leaves and salt. Cook for 1–2 minutes
longer before adding the quartered eggs.

Served alone, this makes a meal for three, but can easily be
'stretched' to feed four or five adults if served on steamed
rice (see page 44) and accompanied with Indian breads.

Desserts & Treats

While not essential, a dessert or sweet treat after a main course can raise a meal to new heights! Whether you are looking for a family favourite, something stylish for friends, or just a morsel to serve with coffee, you are sure to find something tempting here.

Instant Strawberry Ice Cream

This ice cream is ready to eat one minute after you start making it. Either freeze the fruit or berry of your choice in packets containing 2 cups, or buy frozen berries. You must use free-flow, hard frozen berries cut in thumbnail size cubes when making the ice cream.

FOR 3–4 SERVINGS:
2 cups frozen (diced) free-flow strawberries
½ cup icing sugar
about ½ cup chilled cream, milk or yoghurt

Chop berries into 5mm–1cm cubes. Fruit MUST be frozen hard, free-flow and in small pieces when used. Tip into food processor bowl. Work quickly to keep fruit very cold. Process with metal chopping blade until fruit is finely chopped (10–20 seconds). This is a noisy operation. Without delay, add the icing sugar and process briefly until mixed.

With machine running, add the chilled liquid of your choice through the feed-tube in a fine stream, until a smooth, frozen cream has formed. The amount needed varies from batch to batch. Stop as soon as the mixture is evenly textured and creamy.

Serve ice cream made with chilled milk or yoghurt immediately. Ice cream made with cream may be frozen for later use if desired.

VARIATION: Replace icing sugar with low calorie sweetener if desired. Experiment with other berries, berry mixtures and cubed raw fruit.

NOTE: Berries with many seeds are not successful and bland fruits do not make memorable ice cream.

Sugar-dusted Crisps

These are fun, deliciously crunchy, and a little different! They are especially good served with ice cream or other soft textured foods.

Use fresh or thawed wonton skins. Leave them whole, or cut them diagonally or in strips. Heat about a cup of grapeseed or canola oil, preferably in a wok (or in a smallish pot), until it is hot enough to fry a piece of wonton in 40–50 seconds.

Drop in wontons one, two or three at a time, depending on size of pieces and the container. Turn if necessary to lightly brown all sides. When frying whole wontons, pinch them into interesting folds with tongs while they cook.

When evenly golden brown, drain on paper towels, dust with sieved icing sugar and serve as soon as possible (or store in airtight plastic bags).

Raspberry Meringue Cream ▾

Raspberries give tartness, flavour and a very pretty colour to this easily assembled, summery dessert. (Exact proportions are not essential.)

FOR 4-6 SERVINGS:
about 125g "bought" meringues
about 250g frozen or fresh raspberries
300ml cream, lightly whipped
½ tsp vanilla essence

Cut or break meringues into chunky 1cm cubes. Do not crumble finely.

Thaw frozen raspberries, putting a few perfect whole berries aside for a garnish. Break and mash the rest into smaller pieces as they become softer. (Larger amounts of berries make a pudding with a stronger fruit flavour.) The pudding is best assembled when the berries are almost completely thawed. If using fresh berries, slightly mash them with the back of a spoon. Do not purée the fresh or frozen berries.

In a large bowl, beat the cream with the vanilla until the mixture is just thick enough so that you cannot pour it from the bowl. Take care not to overbeat the cream until it looks dry. Using a spatula or stirrer, fold all the meringue pieces through the whipped cream, then fold the raspberries (and any raspberry juice) fairly evenly through the mixture. Leave a few streaks, since these look pretty. Spoon the mixture carefully into individual dishes and serve immediately or refrigerate up to an hour or so. Serve cold, garnished with reserved berries and mint sprigs if available.

Home-made Meringues

In a large mixer bowl combine the whites of 2 large eggs, a pinch of salt, ½ cup caster sugar and ½ teaspoon of vanilla. Beat together for about 10 minutes or until stiff with peaks that just fold over at the tip when the beater is lifted from them. Shape into about 24 small meringues on a Teflon liner or baking paper. Bake without browning at 100°C for 1–1½ hours, until a meringue, when cooled for 5 minutes, is dry right through. Store cooled meringues in airtight plastic bags or other suitable containers until required (for up to a month).

Kiwifruit Tiramisu ▲

Contrasting layers of diced kiwifruit, coffee-soaked cake and marscapone-cream served in tall glasses ensure this easy dessert looks as good as it tastes.

FOR ABOUT 8 SERVINGS:
8–12 Zespri Green kiwifruit
caster sugar (optional)
300g (about 1¼ cups) marscapone
1 Tbsp brandy, coffee or orange liqueur
¼ cup caster sugar
1 cup cream, lightly whipped
4 tsp instant coffee
1 cup sugar
½ cup hot water
400–500g Madeira cake, cubed
shaved or grated chocolate to garnish

Peel the Zespri Green kiwifruit, then quarter them lengthways and cut into 7–10mm thick slices. Sprinkle with a little caster sugar to sweeten slightly if desired.

Put the marscapone in a large bowl and stir in the brandy or liqueur and caster sugar (this should soften it nicely), then fold in the lightly whipped cream. Cover and set aside until required.

Stir the instant coffee, sugar and water together in a small pot (or microwave bowl). Bring to the boil and simmer for 2–3 minutes until the sugar dissolves. While the syrup cools, cut the Madeira cake into 1–2cm cubes. Place cubes in a shallow dish or tray and drizzle with the syrup, turning them gently so most sides are covered with syrup.

Arrange the sponge, kiwifruit and cream in alternate layers in individual glasses or other containers. Vary the order as you please. If you put sponge at the bottom it soaks up any excess liquid nicely. If you finish with a layer or dollop of the cream mixture, it looks great garnished with a little shaved or grated dark chocolate. (If desired, you can assemble these, except for the final layer, up to 8 hours in advance, then just cover and refrigerate until required.)

Passionfruit Panacotta with Grilled Nectarines ▶

This quickly made dessert must be prepared several hours before you need it – overnight is good. We like it with ripe nectarines grilled at the last minute, or with fresh berries.

FOR FOUR ½ CUP SERVINGS:
¼ cup orange juice
3 level tsp gelatine
¼ cup sugar
¼ cup passionfruit pulp
1¼ cups cream
½ cup milk
1 tsp vanilla essence

Stir orange juice and gelatine together in a small container and leave to soften. Meanwhile, stir the sugar and passionfruit pulp together in a pot over low heat until the sugar dissolves. Take off heat and stir in the softened gelatine until it melts. Stir the cream into the warm mixture. Add the milk and vanilla. Stand the pot in a bigger bowl containing cold water and ice blocks and cool, stirring frequently until mixture thickens enough to hold up the passionfruit seeds. Pour into four clean, wetted glasses, plastic glasses or bowls, each of which holds about ½ a cup. Refrigerate for at least 4 hours.

When panacottas have set well, warm the sides and base of each container briefly by dipping in warm water. Tilt container and run a thin knife blade between each pudding and its container to help the pudding slip out, then turn out onto flat plates. Pour a little bought passionfruit yoghurt topping or flavouring, or homemade coulis (see following recipe) over each dessert just before serving with the grilled nectarines, and the rest of the coulis in a bowl.

Passionfruit Coulis

Chop two peeled nectarines or peaches into thin slices. Simmer in ¼ cup of orange juice for 5–10 minutes, then purée fruit and liquid until smooth. Stir in 2–4 tablespoons of passionfruit pulp (or topping), leave to cool, then thin to pouring consistency with extra juice if necessary.

Grilled Nectarines

Preheat grill five minutes before starting to cook. Halve ripe nectarines (one per person) and remove stones. Dip cut surface in a little orange or lemon juice. Place cut side up on a shallow pan lined with lightly buttered foil. Sprinkle fruit with sugar, allowing about a teaspoon per half. Grill 10–12cm from heat until cut surface is golden brown, probably about 5 minutes.

Rhubarb, Rhubarb, Rhubarb ▾

Rhubarb Sago

Microwaved sago puddings do not burn on the bottom. Sago makes sour fruit (like rhubarb) less acid, and often more popular with children. Look for sago in Oriental food stores if you cannot find it in your supermarket.

FOR 4 SERVINGS:

¼ cup sago
1½ cups hot tap water
500g (4 cups) chopped rhubarb
½ cup sugar

Put the sago and water in a covered microwave dish about 23cm in diameter. Cover and microwave on high (100%) power for 4 minutes or until the sago mixture has thickened and nearly all the grains of sago have gone clear.

Stir in the rhubarb, chopped into 1cm lengths, and the sugar. Cover again, microwave on high (100%) power for

three minutes, then stir well. Cover and cook for 3–4 minutes longer until all rhubarb is hot. Leave to stand for 5 minutes – the rhubarb should finish cooking in this time. Serve warm or cold, alone, with yoghurt, or lightly whipped or runny cream.

Stewed Rhubarb

Chop 500g of rhubarb into 2–4cm lengths and put aside. In a large pot with a close-fitting lid, bring to the boil ½ cup white or brown sugar, ½ cup water, and the finely grated rind of one lemon or orange, or about a teaspoon of freshly grated root ginger, stirring until the sugar dissolves. Lie the rhubarb flat in the syrup, heat quickly until the syrup starts to bubble again, then turn very low, cover with the lid and simmer very gently for 4–6 minutes, until the rhubarb feels tender. Take off the heat, cool the pot in a sink of very cold water and serve warm or cold, with unsweetened yoghurt or runny cream.

Rhubarb Fool

Chop 500g rhubarb in 5mm–1cm pieces, put in a pot with ½ cup white or brown sugar mixed with 2 level teaspoons of cornflour or custard powder, and ¼ cup of water or orange juice. Stir over medium heat until the rhubarb and its sauce thickens, then simmer gently for 5 minutes, stirring often. As soon as the rhubarb breaks up stand the pot in very cold water and mash rhubarb with a potato masher or, for a smoother mixture, purée in a blender or food processor. Whip about ½ cup of cream until it will not pour from the bowl, then fold the whipped cream and cold rhubarb together, spoon into 4 glasses or bowls and refrigerate for at least half an hour before serving.

Creamy Custards – Variations on a Theme ▸

Microwaved custards are smooth and velvety, and may be refrigerated in covered containers for several days.

Vanilla Custard

FOR 4 SERVINGS:

¼ cup custard powder or cornflour
¼ cup sugar
1 egg
2 cups (500ml) milk (any type)
1 tsp vanilla essence
1–2 Tbsp butter

Stir custard powder or cornflour and sugar together in a microwave jug or bowl about 12–14cm across. Break in the egg and add the milk and vanilla. Beat or whisk well, then cook uncovered on high (100%) power for 3 minutes, take out, beat or whisk again, and microwave 1 minute more. Stir in the butter which has been cut into small cubes, and cook for another minute. Repeat, stirring then cooking for a minute, until the custard thickens. Stir well, then lie a plastic bag on the custard, so it covers the whole surface, and no skin can form. Cool the container in cold water, or in the refrigerator or at room temperature, or serve warm.

Caramel Custard

Follow the previous recipe, using brown or dark brown sugar to replace white sugar. Taste while still hot, after it thickens, and stir in 1 or 2 extra tablespoons of (dark) brown sugar if you like.

Chocolate Custard

Add 3 LEVELLED measuring tablespoons of cocoa and ¼ cup of extra sugar to the custard powder or cornflour and sugar mixture and proceed as for vanilla custard.

Banana Custard

Let vanilla or caramel custard cool until you can hold the sides of the container, then slice in one or two bananas, and stir to mix.

Trifle

Put cubes of sponge cake in the bottom of a serving dish (or individual dishes), drizzle with syrup from the fruit to be used, and/or sherry to taste. Top with raspberry jam and drained, cooked sliced peaches, mango, etc. Cover with a layer of vanilla custard and top with whipped cream.

VARIATION: Just before serving, sprinkle with crushed praline (page 90).

Over the Top ▼

Raspberry Sauce

1 cup of fresh or frozen raspberries
2 Tbsp caster sugar
1 tsp cornflour

Purée or mash all ingredients together and bring to the boil so that the sauce thickens slightly. Serve warm or cold, over ice cream etc.

Caramel Sauce

25g butter
½ cup dark or regular brown sugar
¼ cup golden syrup
¼ cup water
pinch of salt
400g can sweetened condensed milk
1 tsp vanilla essence

Melt the butter in a medium-sized pot. Add brown sugar (darker sugar gives more colour and flavour), syrup, water and salt, and bring to the boil, stirring until the sugar has dissolved and the mixture bubbles furiously. Lower heat, add the condensed milk and vanilla, and stir over low heat until well mixed, then take off stove. Serve hot, warm or cold, thinning with hot water, sherry, spirits or liqueurs if sauce is too thick. Use straight away or refrigerate, microwaving to warm when needed.

Chocolate Sauce

2 Tbsp water
¼ cup sugar
100g dark or milk chocolate
¼ cup cream

Heat the water and sugar in a microwave dish on high (100%) power for 1½–2 minutes, stirring after a minute, until the sugar has dissolved completely and the syrup has boiled. Break the chocolate into squares or smaller pieces, and tip into the hot syrup. Leave to stand for a minute, then stir until dissolved. Heat for one or more five second bursts only if necessary. Serve warm.

Banana Splits

Kids of all ages love banana splits! For maximum impact, serve them in long sundae dishes, and don't forget the trimmings!

For each banana split, cut a banana lengthwise and place, cut surfaces facing in and ends facing up, on a long sundae dish. Put 2–3 scoops of ice cream between the halved banana, drizzle with chocolate, caramel or raspberry sauce, top with cherries or chopped nuts, and decorate with wafers.

Decadent Chocolate Fondue ▲

People of all ages seem to enjoy dipping into a communal pot of chocolate fondue. The dipping fruit disappears like magic, so have plenty!

200–250g dark or milk chocolate
½ cup cream
grated rind of 1 orange or
   1–2 Tbsp brandy, rum or liqueur (optional)

Break the chocolate into squares or small pieces, and place in a flat-bottomed microwave dish. Pour the cream over the chocolate. For orange flavouring, finely grate orange rind into the mixture. (A microplane grater does a great job.)

Microwave uncovered on high (100%) power for 2 minutes, leave to stand for 1 minute, then stir until the chocolate and cream are evenly mixed. If any lumps remain, microwave again in 20 second bursts, until lumps disappear when stirred. Stir in spirits, if using.

Pour warm mixture into one or more serving dishes, or rewarm and serve later.

Pile generous amounts of bite-sized pieces of fruit on a flat plate around the hot chocolate dip. (Prepare the fruit ahead and refrigerate in plastic bags, if desired.) Suitable ripe, raw dipping fruits include: apricots, apples, bananas, cherries, grapes, green and yellow kiwifruit, melons, nectarines, oranges, nashi, pawpaw, peaches, pears, plums, pineapple, and strawberries.

NOTE: Two-pronged cocktail forks hold fruit pieces in place better than skewers. Have plenty of paper napkins on hand!

Star Attractions ▶

For something so simple to make, these light pastry shapes are an excellent and spectacular way to end a meal.

FOR 4 SERVINGS:
1 sheet pre-rolled frozen flaky pastry (about 150g), thawed
2 cups berries, single variety or mixed strawberries, raspberries and blueberries
1–2 Tbsp caster sugar
2 Tbsp orange juice
250–300ml cream
1–2 Tbsp caster sugar
finely grated rind of ½ an orange
2–3 drops vanilla essence
icing sugar to dust

Preheat the oven to 200°C. While the oven heats, cut the pastry shapes. Star shapes look extra special (just cut by hand around a cardboard template if you don't have a star cutter big enough), but if you're in a rush then rounds, rectangles (you can get six servings from a sheet with rectangles), or any other shape for that matter, taste just as good. Arrange the pastry on a baking sheet and chill until the oven is ready, then bake for 5–6 minutes until puffed and golden brown. Remove from the oven and cool on a wire rack. (You can do this well in advance if you like.)

Hull and halve or quarter any large strawberries, then place the fruit in a medium-sized bowl. Sprinkle in the sugar (start with the smaller amount and add more if required) and orange juice, then stir gently to combine.

Pour the cream into a large bowl, add sugar to taste, then add the orange rind and vanilla. Beat or whisk until softly whipped (the mixture will just hold its shape but does not look dry).

Assemble just before serving by carefully splitting the pastry shapes into two layers. Place the bottom layer on a flattish plate or bowl and cover with a generous spoonful of the berries. Top the berries with a blob of cream, then carefully place on the pastry cap. Dust with icing sugar (put a little in a fine sieve and tap or shake gently) and serve.

Poached Fruit in Chardonnay Syrup ▼

In cold weather this delicious dried fruit mixture is a reminder of summer! Serve it straight away or refrigerate in a covered jar for several days. Enjoy it warm or cold, alone, or with a slice of plain cake, an after dinner treat, or a selection of cheeses.

FOR ABOUT 4 SERVINGS:
1 cup orange juice
1 cup water
1 cup Chardonnay
½ cup sugar
1–2 cinnamon sticks
3–4 cloves
400g Alison's Choice (dried) Orchard Fruits*
2–3 Tbsp skin-on or blanched almonds (optional)

Heat the first six ingredients until the mixture is simmering and the sugar has dissolved, then add all the dried fruit

except the dates and simmer for about 10 minutes until the fruit has plumped up nicely. Add dates about 30 seconds before taking off heat. Transfer the fruit, with syrup to cover, to a lidded jar, cool, then refrigerate up to a week or, if using immediately, place in a serving bowl. When required, warm slightly if preferred. Serve fruit with a little syrup.

VARIATION: Replace orange juice with 1 cup of water, the juice of a lemon and a curl of lemon rind if preferred. During storage, fruit should be covered with syrup.

*Look for this fruit mixture in Alison's Choice Bulk Self-selection bins at New World supermarkets OR replace with the same total weight of a mixture of: dried apricots, pears, apple rings, prunes, crystallised pineapple pieces, and crystallised ginger.

Fresh Fruit Ideas

A mixture of three or four fruits looks much more inviting than just one or two. When making a selection consider contrasting colours and textures as well as flavours. Watermelon pieces, large fat blueberries and whole grapes always look great. Large, chunky pieces of fruit look better than small cubes.

Sprinkle cut fruit, especially strawberries, lightly with caster sugar a few minutes before serving, to form juices which glaze the fruit.

Pour chilled Chardonnay (or other interesting) syrup over fresh fruit. Serve cold. Pour sparkling wine over berries in glasses. Garnish with a mint sprig.

Add extra flavour to fruit syrups by adding finely grated orange, lemon rind, fresh root ginger or mint leaves. Try adding a few drops of real vanilla flavour, or try star anise, a cinnamon stick, or freshly grated nutmeg for variety.

Easy Apple Tartlets

If you use pre-rolled pastry sheets for these, the most complicated step in the preparation of these delicious little tartlets is peeling and slicing a couple of apples!

FOR 4 SERVINGS:
1 sheet pre-rolled flaky pastry
2 Tbsp walnut or pecan pieces
1 Tbsp caster sugar
½ tsp cinnamon
2 medium apples (Granny Smith or Braeburn)
3–4 Tbsp apricot jam, warmed

Sit the pastry on a lightly floured board to thaw and turn the oven on to 190°C (180°C if using fanbake).

Measure the nuts, sugar and cinnamon into a food processor or blender and process until the nuts are finely chopped.

Peel, then halve and core the apples. Lie each half on a board and slice crossways into slices 2–3mm thick. (Depending on the size of the apple you should have 15–20 slices.)

Cut a 2cm wide strip from one side of the pastry sheet so you are left with a rectangle. Cut this into four (equally sized) smaller rectangles and arrange these on a baking sheet. Without cutting right through, run a sharp knife 1cm in from the edge of each rectangle so it marks out a frame. Spread 1–2 tsp of the sugar-nut mixture over each piece of pastry, leaving the border clear, then carefully fan out a sliced apple half on each.

Bake for 15 minutes or until the pastry is golden brown. Leave to stand for 5–10 minutes, then brush each tartlet with a little warmed apricot jam (heat jam for about 30 seconds in the microwave) to glaze, then serve.

Spicy Apple Pie

Using ready-rolled pastry and a food processor, you can make this deliciously spicy pie (with the flavour of Christmas mincemeat) very quickly.

FOR 6-8 SERVINGS:
2 sheets pre-rolled flaky or puff pastry
½ cup ground almonds (optional)
2 Tbsp plain flour
½ cup raisins or sultanas
¼ cup brown sugar
2 tsp cinnamon
2 tsp mixed spice
¼ tsp ground cloves
1 egg
4 apples (Granny Smith or Braeburn)

Preheat the oven to 200°C with the rack just below the middle. On a floured surface, roll the (fresh or thawed) pastry sheets out more thinly, about 5cm bigger each way. Place one rolled pastry sheet on a baking tray on a non-stick liner or baking paper. Measure all the dry ingredients into a large bowl, mix well with your fingers, and put aside. Beat the egg in a small bowl with a fork.

A food processor does not chop well when overfull, so it is faster and more efficient to mix the filling in two batches. Slice 2 apples, skin and all, into a full-sized food processor fitted with chopping blade. Each apple should be in 10–12 slices. Process in bursts until apple pieces are in small, even chunks but not mushy. Tip into the large bowl with the mixed dry ingredients. Process the remaining apples in the same way. Tip into the bowl, add about a third of the beaten egg, then mix the filling well, using your hand. Pile the filling onto the pastry on the tray, then spread it evenly over the pastry leaving a 2cm strip all round the edge. Brush this strip with some of the remaining egg. Put the second pastry sheet over the apple and pastry, pressing the edges firmly together. Trim the edges evenly without cutting the liner. With a sharp knife, cut a pattern of slashes diagonally across the top crust. Brush the pastry top with the remaining egg.

Bake about 20 minutes at 200°C or until golden brown top and bottom. Dust with icing sugar and serve warm or reheated, with ice cream or lightly whipped cream if desired.

VARIATION: For 2–3 servings, use only one sheet of pastry and make the pie rectangular rather than square. Make half the filling, and use 1 egg, mixing half of it in with the apple. Fold one side of the pastry square over the filling which has been spread on the other half. Seal the open edges and bake as above.

Filo Tartlets with Lemon Cloud Filling ▲

Filo pastry makes quick, crisp, light containers for all sorts of delicious fillings! This one is light and lemony – and made in seconds!

You can make these in small pans for one-bite mouthfuls, or in medium or large muffin or patty pans. Use a piece of thin paper or a tissue to work out what size squares of filo you will need to go across the bottoms and up the sides of your chosen baking pans.

Preheat oven to 180°C. Place a sheet of filo on a dry surface, brush it lightly with unflavoured oil, then cover with another sheet. Using your paper guide, cut two squares for each tart. Take two of the sandwiched squares, place one over the other so the corners form eight-pointed stars, then press them lightly into non-stick sprayed pans. Make as many as required, sandwiching more filo sheets after you have shaped those cut out previously.

Bake for 5–8 minutes, until pastry is evenly golden brown.

Lower temperature if corners brown too fast. Take from pans and cool on a rack.

Just before serving, fill tartlets with precooked mixtures and dust with sifted icing sugar. (The icing sugar on moist fillings will disappear.)

LEMON CLOUD FILLING: Make this while the cases cook. Fold together lightly whipped unsweetened cream with good quality lemon honey. Use proportions to suit, starting with half the volume of lemon honey as whipped cream. Top with fresh strawberries if you like. Try passionfruit honey, too.

OTHER FILLINGS: Use the Star Attraction filling (page 74) or cold custard (page 70), or cream cheese beaten with icing sugar and vanilla, brandy or liqueur to taste. Top with sugared or glazed fresh berries or glazed cooked fruit, ready-made cheesecake topping or Christmas mincemeat.

Filo Pear Triangles ▼

These delicious little triangles are flavoured with pears, ginger and nuts.

FOR 4 SERVINGS:
½ slice toast bread
¼ cup roasted cashews
6 pieces crystallised ginger
3 medium-sized firm pears
2 Tbsp sugar
¼ cup sour cream
1 egg yolk
6 sheets filo pastry
oil for brushing

Preheat oven to 180°C. Food process the bread, cashews and ginger until roughly chopped. Add unpeeled pears which have been quartered and cored, then cut in chunks, the sugar, sour cream and egg yolk. Process briefly in bursts, until pear pieces are pea-sized.

Take 3 sheets of the filo pastry and, working quickly on a dry bench, brush the upper side of each one lightly with oil (the whole surface need not be covered). Layer these three sheets, then cut into four even strips crosswise. Put an eighth of the filling at the end of one strip. Fold the end over to form a triangle, then continue folding to encase the filling completely, always forming triangles. Repeat with remaining pastry and filling.

Brush the folded parcels with a little more oil and bake on an oven tray covered with Teflon or baking paper for about 15 minutes, until golden brown. Serve warm, dusted with icing sugar, with whipped cream or yoghurt.

SPICY APPLE TRIANGLES: Replace pear filling with the apple filling on page 77.

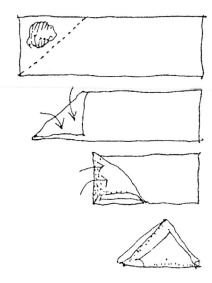

Orange Syrup Cakes ▶

This really easy cake recipe has become a stand by dessert for our entire family! These little cakes are good as is, but if you've got time to soak them with the syrup, it transforms them into a really special dessert.

FOR 6 INDIVIDUAL CAKES:
1 cup sugar
½ cup canola (or other) oil
2 large eggs
finely grated rind of 1 medium orange
½ cup freshly squeezed orange juice
1 tsp vanilla essence
½ tsp salt
1½ cups self-raising flour

ORANGE SYRUP:
¾ cup hot water
¾ cup sugar
finely grated rind of ½ an orange

Preheat the oven to 180°C (or 170°C if using fanbake). Measure sugar, oil, eggs and grated rind into a food processor and blend until pale and creamy. Add orange juice and vanilla and whiz again, then sieve in the salt and flour.

Mix just enough to make a fairly smooth batter.

Divide the batter evenly (about ½ cup in each) between six non-stick sprayed plain or fancy muffin tins or other moulds (each should hold 1 cup when full). Bake for 12–15 minutes or until the cakes are golden brown and a skewer poked into the middle of a cake comes out clean.

While the cakes cook prepare the syrup by mixing the hot water, sugar and grated orange rind together in a small microwave bowl or pot. Heat for about 3 minutes on high (100%) power, stirring occasionally, until the mixture boils and the sugar dissolves.

Remove cakes from the oven. Stand for 2–3 minutes before inverting onto a plate or tray and removing the tins. Drizzle the syrup evenly over the bottom and sides of the hot cakes (about 2 Tbsp per little cake).

Leave to stand for at least an hour (overnight is good if possible), before cutting and serving with lightly whipped cream, ice cream or yoghurt.

Fruity Steamed Pudding

This pudding has a lovely flavour and wonderful aroma. Make it for a quick winter pudding or dress it up for Christmas dinner! It contains no flour, butter or oil, and is quick to mix. Reheat leftovers or eat cold, as with fruit cake.

FOR 4–6 SERVINGS:
1¼ cups instant rolled oats
1 cup milk
2 household dessertspoons golden syrup
500g (4 cups) good quality mixed fruit
1 tsp cinnamon
1 tsp mixed spice
½ tsp ground cloves
½ tsp lemon essence
½ tsp salt
1 large egg
1 tsp baking soda

First of all, measure the oats into a fairly large mixing bowl, pour the milk over them, and leave to stand for a few minutes while you get out everything else. Put the dried fruit in a sieve and run boiling or very hot water over it. Drain well and tip it on top of the oats, without stirring. Drizzle the measured golden syrup over the hot fruit so it softens. Add the flavourings, salt and egg, then mix everything together thoroughly with a fork. Measure the baking soda, tip it into your palm, press with the back of a spoon to make sure there are no lumps, then sprinkle it over the mixture and stir in well.

Lightly but evenly spray a six-cup microwave ring pan with non-stick spray. Pour the wet-looking pudding mixture into this and cover the top lightly with a paper towel or a piece of greaseproof or baking paper. Place it on an upturned dinner plate (so the base of the pudding cooks faster) and microwave at medium-high (70%) power for 15 minutes. Leave to stand for 5 minutes before turning out onto a flat plate. (This is a little faster than making individual puddings.)

OR spray 6-8 teacups or cup-sized ramekins lightly but evenly with non-stick spray. Divide mixture between these, so each is about ¾ full. Level the tops, and cover loosely with squares of baking paper. Place in a circle on the turntable, about 5cm from the outer edge, and microwave for 12–14 minutes on medium-high (70%) power, until the tops of the puddings have set and seem cooked, although they will still feel soft. Leave to stand for 5 minutes before turning out. Pudding colour darkens on standing. If they don't come out easily when upturned, slip a thin bladed knife down the side of each so they slide out.

Serve with lightly sweetened whipped cream (plain, or flavoured with a little rum or brandy), bought or home-made custard (page 70), or with rum or brandy butter.

Bourbon Street Bread Pudding ▶

Forget your previous thoughts about bread puddings! This one, with its wonderful sauce, is rich, sinfully delicious, and addictive!

FOR 4 SERVINGS:
25g butter
¾ cup milk
¼ cup cream
½ cup sugar
1 large egg
white of 1 large egg
1 tsp vanilla essence
½ tsp cinnamon or mixed spice
½ tsp grated nutmeg
75g very dry bread (2 bread rolls)
¼ cup sultanas or currants

SAUCE:
50g butter
¾ cup icing sugar
yolk of 1 large egg
2–3 Tbsp rum, whisky or bourbon

In a large bowl melt the butter on high (100%) power for about a minute. Stir in all remaining ingredients except the bread and dried fruit, and mix well, using a fork. Add the bread, crumbled or cut in 1cm cubes, and the dried fruit. Leave to stand for a few minutes while the bread softens, then mix again. The mixture should be firm enough to keep a rounded shape in four microwave-proof bowls, ramekins or cups. Spoon in mixture so each container is no more than three-quarters full. Microwave uncovered at medium (50%) power for 8–10 minutes or until firm. Serve warm, with the warm sauce drizzled over the top.

SAUCE: In a medium-sized bowl melt the butter on high (100%) power for 1 minute. Beat in icing sugar and egg yolk. Microwave for 30 seconds or until the liquid bubbles around the edges. Cool, then stir in the whisky, rum or bourbon.

Instant Coffee Gateau ▼

This makes an excellent dessert for entertaining, since it can be prepared the night before you need it. Leftovers may be enjoyed for a couple of days after this, too.

Avoid the temptation to serve this cake only a few hours after you have made it, or you will be disappointed. It needs at least 12 hours to absorb moisture from the cream and syrup.

FOR 8 SERVINGS:

1 unfilled sponge sandwich 20-23cm across or
   one layer of slab sponge, 30 x 25cm
1 Tbsp instant coffee
¾ cup sugar
¼ cup water
½ tsp rum or brandy essence or 2 Tbsp rum or brandy
1½ cups cream, whipped
4–6 Zespri Green or Gold kiwifruit
about ½ cup chopped walnuts or slivered toasted almonds

Split each layer of sponge, making two thinner layers. Use three layers for this cake. (Layers may be patched, and unused sponge frozen for later use.) Use slab cake to make a long, rectangular log to cut in slices.

Boil instant coffee, sugar and water together, stirring constantly until sugar has dissolved completely, then simmer for 2 minutes, cool and add essence or spirits. Whip the cream until it is just thick enough not to pour from the bowl.

Place a layer of sponge on a serving dish, drizzle or brush a quarter of the syrup over it, then top with half the thinly peeled, sliced kiwifruit and no more than a quarter of the whipped cream. Drizzle or brush the same quantity of syrup over the next layer of cake while it is lying on the working surface, then place it, coffee side down, over the cream.

Repeat, using the remaining syrup and fruit, and the third layer of cake, then spread the sides and top of the cake with as much of the remaining cream as necessary. Sprinkle nuts over sides (and top if desired) of the cake. Cover carefully and refrigerate for at least 12 hours (preferably 24) before serving. Cut in wedges or slices to serve, with extra fruit to garnish if you like.

VARIATION: Decorate the top of the gateau with overlapping slices of fruit just before serving OR replace kiwifruit with sliced strawberries OR prepare gateau as above but without putting fruit in the filling. Pile grapes or berries on top if desired.

Black Forest Roll ▲

This easy and reliable sponge roll has been a stand by in our house for decades, celebrating many birthdays and special occasions. We can take the cake from the oven less than twenty minutes after we start mixing.

3 large eggs
½ cup sugar
¼ tsp salt
½ cup flour
2 Tbsp cocoa
1 tsp baking powder
1 Tbsp boiling water

Filling, see following

Heat oven to 230°C (or 220°C fanbake), with the rack just below the centre of oven. With an electric beater, beat eggs, sugar and salt together in a fairly large bowl, until mixture is thick, creamy and pale. (Use room temperature eggs and don't hurry the beating.) Meanwhile, line the bottom and sides of a fairly large (about 22 x 30cm) sponge roll tin with a piece of baking paper cut at the corners where the edges fold up.

Measure the flour, cocoa and baking powder into a sieve over a piece of paper, then lift paper, return mixture to the sieve, and sift it on to the thick egg mixture. Fold in carefully but thoroughly until no pockets of dry ingredients remain. Add the boiling water and fold it in too, then spread the thick mixture evenly in the lined tin.

Bake for 7–10 minutes or until the centre springs back when pressed lightly. (Take care not to cook longer than necessary or the sponge will shrink.)

While sponge roll cooks, lightly butter another piece of baking paper or a large Teflon liner. Sprinkle caster sugar evenly over this, shaking off excess. Quickly turn the cooked cake out onto this surface, bottom up. Lift off the baking paper and cool the sponge on the sugared surface on a cooling rack.

FILLING AND DECORATING: When cooled to room temperature, spread with raspberry jam, then whipped rum cream. (Beat 1 cup of cream with ¼ cup icing sugar and 1–2 Tbsp rum until thick.) Over this sprinkle well-drained canned or bottled cherries or about a cup of fresh or thawed raspberries.

Roll up, starting from a short end, lifting the paper or liner to help you. Keep the paper/liner rolled around the roll until you are ready to serve it, then serve, join-side down, as is, or dusted with icing sugar. Add chocolate or white chocolate curls for extra decoration, if you like.

VARIATION: If preferred, cut cream-topped sponge in two or three pieces and layer these, instead of forming a roll.

Quick Chocolate Brownies ▼

Brownies and vanilla ice cream are a delicious traditional combination. Microwaved brownies are soft textured when served the day they are made, and become firmer on standing. They are good both ways – just different!

FOR 6 LARGE OR 12 REGULAR BROWNIES:
½ cup canola or other unflavoured oil
2 large eggs
1 cup sugar
1 tsp vanilla essence
½ tsp salt
½ cup self-raising flour
½ cup plain flour
¼ cup cocoa
¼–½ cup chopped walnuts (optional)

Measure the oil, eggs, sugar, vanilla and salt into a medium-sized bowl and beat well with a fork.

Measure the flours and cocoa into a sieve over the bowl. Sift into the mixture and fold everything together evenly, using a stirrer or rubber scraper. Stir in the nuts if using.

Line a 20cm square (or 21 x 15cm rectangular microwave container) with straight sides at least 6cm high, with a piece of cling film. Tip in the prepared mixture and spread evenly.

Cover with a non-stick liner or baking paper. (Covering is important for even rising and cooking.)

Stand the dish on an inverted plate so it is at least 1cm above the cooking surface. Microwave on high (100%) power for 4–7 minutes, checking every minute after 4 minutes. Do not worry if the surface looks rather uneven, but don't take the brownies out of the microwave until they are dry on top. Cool in cooking container, then turn out onto a cutting board. When cold, cut into bars or other shapes.

Dust the top with icing sugar, or turn the cut pieces in sifted icing sugar so all surfaces are covered. Serve with vanilla ice cream.

NOTE: If the top is not covered during cooking, brownies will take longer to cook and the top may not cook (and rise) evenly. We use a lidded rectangular plastic storage container (without its lid) to cook our brownies, and find it very successful.

VARIATION: If preferred, bake brownies in a 20cm square baking-paper lined pan at 180°C for 20–30 minutes or until a toothpick comes out clean.

Shortcut Apple Crumble ▲

Unbelievably quick and easy, this crumble has only two ingredients. Proportions need not be exact. They are listed just to give you an idea of quantities.

FOR 2 SERVINGS:
(USE DOUBLE QUANTITIES FOR 4 PEOPLE)

1–2 cups hot, cooked, unsweetened apple or a 400g can of diced apple
¾–1 cup muesli*

* Use Alison's Apricot and Almond Muesli, Alison's Cranberry Crunch, or Alison's Decadent Delight (in a foil pack), available from New World stores. (Only muesli with a crumbled biscuity texture works for this pudding.)

Preheat the oven to 170–180°C. Heat contents of a 400g can of diced apple in a microwave dish in a microwave or in a pot. Add a little orange juice if it seems dry, and heat until warmed through.

Put the hot, cooked apple (and juice) in a well-sprayed baking dish (as for a traditional apple crumble). Sprinkle evenly with muesli, pushing down visible dried fruit into the apple, so it does not burn. Cover loosely with a piece of foil or a Teflon liner and bake for 10 minutes, then uncover and bake for 5–10 minutes longer. Watch that the topping browns only to the golden brown stage, but not too much.

Serve warm with ice cream, sour or fresh cream, plain yoghurt or custard (page 70).

NOTE: For home-cooked apple, coarsely grate (or chop in a food processor) unpeeled Granny Smiths or other apples. Heat in a covered microwave-proof dish (in which the pudding can later be baked), or simmer in a covered pot with ½ cup of orange juice until tender and juicy. (3 cups of raw grated apple yields about 2 cups of cooked apple.)

Rich Mocha Mousse

Serve this deliciously rich mixture in small portions for special occasions!

FOR 8-12 SERVINGS:
500g dark chocolate
½ cup hot water
2 tsp instant coffee
juice & finely grated rind of 2 medium-sized oranges
3 large eggs, separated

Break chocolate into squares. Heat with the water, instant coffee, orange juice and finely grated orange rind in the microwave, uncovered, on defrost (30%) power, for 6–7 minutes or until the chocolate has melted. Stir until smooth. Meanwhile, separate the eggs and beat the whites until they form peaks which turn over at the tips when the beater is lifted. Using a whisk, beat the egg yolks into the hot, melted chocolate mixture, then fold in the beaten whites.

Divide mixture between 8–12 small dishes, glasses or coffee cups. Refrigerate for at least 2 hours before serving as is, or with lightly whipped cream, chocolate curls, etc.

NOTE: Refrigerate up to 2 days. With time it will be firmer (but still very good).

Apricot Balls

rind of ½–1 orange
½ cup caster sugar
250g New Zealand* dried apricots, chopped
¼ cup orange juice
about 1¾ cups fine desiccated coconut

Remove orange rind with potato peeler, then chop finely with the sugar in a food processor (use more rind for a stronger flavour). Roughly chop the apricots with kitchen scissors, then pulse them with the orange and sugar until finely chopped. Add the juice and process again. Add a cup of the coconut, process, then add more, stopping when mixture may be rolled in balls with wet hands. Shape, roll in coconut, and refrigerate until firm. If not required immediately, freeze in a covered container for up to three months.

*NZ dried apricots are best – sticky and more tender, with a stronger flavour.

Fail-safe Fudge ▾

250g dark, milk or white chocolate
½ a 400g can sweetened condensed milk
½ tsp vanilla essence
¼–½ cup chopped glacé cherries or dried fruit (optional)
¼–½ cup lightly roasted, chopped almond, walnuts,
   pecans etc. (optional)

Break the chocolate in squares and put it in a medium-sized microwave dish. Add the condensed milk and stir, then heat on medium (50%) power for one minute bursts, stirring between each. Stop as soon as chocolate is completely melted (3-4 minutes in total).

Stir in the vanilla essence and the extras (if any) of your choice, then pour the fudge into a baking paper, Teflon or cling film lined tin and smooth the top if required. We usually use something about 20 x 20cm but for thicker fudge use something smaller.

Cool until firm in the fridge or freezer (this should take about 20-40 minutes, depending on the temperature, thickness etc.), then cut into serving-sized squares and enjoy. Store leftovers in a closed container in the fridge.

Uncooked Coconut Ice ▾

This is easy enough for children to make, but popular with adults too.

2 cups desiccated coconut
2 cups icing sugar
½ a 400g can sweetened condensed milk
1 tsp vanilla essence
¼ tsp raspberry essence (optional)
4–5 drops of red food colouring
extra coconut for coating

Measure coconut and icing sugar into a bowl. Tip in condensed milk and vanilla, then mix well.

Sprinkle some of the extra coconut on a flat sheet of plastic. Press out half the mixture (about 20cm square) on the coconut. Add the raspberry essence and enough food colouring to give a pale pink colour to the mixture left in the bowl, mix in, then shape as previously.

Lay the pink layer on top of the white layer. Sprinkle a little extra coconut on top. Refrigerate for 15 minutes or longer, then cut into squares with a wet knife. Refrigerate until required, and eat after a few hours.

Praline Shards

1 cup sugar
½ cup nuts, such as slivered almonds, chopped macadamias, chopped hazelnuts, peanuts

Heat the sugar in a clean, dry non-stick frypan over a medium heat without stirring at all. As the pan heats and the sugar begins to melt, shake and tilt the pan so it melts evenly. After a few minutes the melted sugar will begin to brown. As soon as the sugar has all melted and is an even light golden-brown colour, add the nuts.

Shake and tilt the pan to combine nuts with the caramel. Taking great care not to burn yourself, carefully pour hot caramel mixture onto a non-stick liner, or baking paper, on an oven tray. Carefully spread out any large clusters of nuts. The mixture should slowly spread out until it is about 5mm thick.

When cool, break the praline into long shards. Serve with coffee or as a garnish for other desserts. Store in clean, dry, airtight containers and use within a week.

NOTE: Do not overcook, as dark caramel develops a bitter taste.

Fabulous Fudge

This microwaved fudge is easier and more reliable than traditionally cooked fudge.

100g butter
1 cup sugar
¼ cup golden syrup
400g can sweetened condensed milk
1 tsp vanilla essence

Mix all ingredients except vanilla in a large bowl resistant to high heat. Microwave on high (100%) power, stirring every 2 minutes until sugar has dissolved, the mixture has bubbled vigorously all over its surface, and a little dropped in cold water forms a soft ball (this is when the mixture which has been dropped in a glass flattens, but stays in a roundish ball after you have shaped it). This usually takes about 10–12 minutes.

Add vanilla and beat for about 5 minutes, until mixture suddenly starts to keep its shape and loses its gloss. Before it sets, quickly turn onto a lightly buttered flat surface or 20cm square pan. When cool and firm, cut into squares.

VARIATION: For Chocolate Fudge, add ¼ cup cocoa powder to the sugar. For Nut Fudge, stir in ¼ cup chopped walnuts after you start beating.

Cherry Truffles ▲

These not-too-rich little balls have been favourites in our house for thirty years!

200g wine biscuits, crushed
1½ cups desiccated coconut
12–20 glacé cherries
100g melted butter
½ a 400g can sweetened condensed milk
1 tsp almond essence (optional)
¼ cup sherry, brandy or Kirsch
extra coconut for coating

Crush broken biscuits finely in a food processor or use a rolling pin to crush biscuits in a plastic bag. Mix the crumbs, coconut and chopped cherries.

Heat the butter in a small pan or microwave bowl until liquid. Take off heat and stir in the condensed milk. Add almond essence if you are not using the Kirsch. Mix in the sherry, brandy or Kirsch, then pour mixture into crumbs and coconut and combine, by hand or in the food processor.

Roll into small balls and coat with extra coconut. Refrigerate or freeze.

Chocolate Coconut Balls ▲

This is our tried and true family favourite chocolate ball recipe.

½ a 250g packet wine biscuits
100g butter
¼ cup cocoa
1 cup icing sugar
½ cup desiccated coconut
2 Tbsp sherry or orange juice
extra coconut for rolling

Put the biscuits in a plastic bag and bang with a rolling pin until completely crushed, or chop the broken biscuits in a food processor.

Soften the butter, taking care not to melt it. Mix with all remaining ingredients (except the extra coconut) in a bowl or food processor. Mix well, then cool the mixture for about 10 minutes in the refrigerator before rolling into small balls.

Roll balls in extra coconut and store in the refrigerator or freezer.

Chocolate Liqueur ▲ Truffles

Ultra rich and smooth, these decadent truffles are wonderful after a special occasion dinner.

150g dark chocolate
2 Tbsp rum, brandy or orange liqueur
2 Tbsp butter
1 egg yolk
¼ cup cocoa

Break chocolate into squares and put in a round microwave-proof or heat-proof glass container with the spirit or liqueur of your choice. Microwave uncovered on defrost (30%) power for 3–4 minutes, or in a bowl over boiling water until the chocolate has melted enough to be mixed smoothly with the liqueur.

Stir in the butter and egg yolk until well combined. (The melted chocolate will melt the butter.) Refrigerate until firm enough to shape into walnut-sized balls, then drop a few at a time into the cocoa in a bowl, and rotate gently until coated. Lift out with a spoon and put on a flat plate or in small cases.

Refrigerate or freeze in a covered container until required. Serve chilled.

Chocolate Dipped ▲ Delights

Chocolate dipped foods always look enticing and are quick and easy to do! Try coating (or partly coating) dried apricots, Brazil and other nuts, grapes and strawberries.

Warm broken squares of dark, milk, or white chocolate in a small microwave bowl, in 30 second bursts, at medium (50%) power, stopping as soon as the chocolate is smooth and semi-liquid when stirred. If necessary, thin the melted chocolate with Kremelta (Copha). Only use a very small amount, as too much will make the chocolate runny and slow down setting. (Add a piece the size of a green pea, then more if needed.) For fast setting, dip dry, chilled foods.

After dipping, hold the food above the container of melted chocolate to catch drips, then cool on a Teflon non-stick liner or a piece of plastic. Refrigerate or stand in a cool place until set. Chocolate dipped strawberries and grapes should be eaten within a few hours but nuts and dried fruits may be refrigerated in a covered container for some weeks.

Say Cheese… ▾

A cheese board is a great alternative (or even an additional finishing touch) to a 'traditional' sweet dessert, and, from a cook's point of view, couldn't be much easier.

Although we are now spoilt for choice, simplicity is often the order of the day for a successful cheese board. Three or perhaps four different cheeses, say a blue (and you can choose from mild or strong to suit your taste), a hardish cheese (like a cheddar, Edam, Gouda, Gruyere etc., or even something smoked) and a soft 'fresh' cheese (a Camembert or Brie) are all that are required. Like red wine, most cheese is better served at room temperature, so it's a good idea to remove it from the fridge (take them out of tight wrappers so they can 'breathe' too) before you sit down to your main course.

Absolute purists assert that the cheese is enough on its own, but some very plain crackers or bread and perhaps a few grapes, some dried fruit and/or a few nuts make good accompaniments too.

Spiced Prunes in Port ▾

Prunes soaked in port are wonderful! They will keep in an unsealed jar in the refrigerator for months, if they get the chance – ready for serving after dinner with cheese, spooned over vanilla ice cream, or snacked on by a deserving cook! The liquid becomes more syrupy with longer storage.

Loosely fill the jar you want to use with good quality prunes. Take them out again, put them in a pot or bowl and cover with boiling water. Leave for 5 minutes – no longer – then pour off and discard the water.

Put the drained prunes back in the jar, adding one or more of the following if you like complex flavours: a piece of cinnamon stick, a few cloves, some juniper berries, crushed cardamom berries, a couple of petals of star anise, and/or a few strips of orange or lemon rind. Leave some space at the top of the jar.

Pour port over the prunes so they are well covered, since they will soak up some port on standing. Cover with a well-fitting lid, and leave at room temperature for 12–36 hours before refrigerating or using.

Index

Knives by Mail Order

For about 20 years Alison has imported her favourite, very sharp kitchen knives from Switzerland. They keep their edges well, are easy to sharpen, a pleasure to use, and make excellent gifts.

VEGETABLE KNIFE $8.00
Ideal for cutting and peeling vegetables, these knives have a straight edged 85mm blade and black (dishwasher-proof) nylon handle. Each knife comes in an individual plastic sheath.

BONING/UTILITY KNIFE $9.50
Excellent for boning chicken and other meats, and/or for general kitchen duties. Featuring a 103mm blade that curves to a point and a dishwasher-proof, black nylon handle, each knife comes in a plastic sheath.

SERRATED KNIFE $9.50
These knives are unbelievably useful. They are perfect for cutting cooked meats, ripe fruit and vegetables, and slicing bread and baking. Treated carefully, these blades stay sharp for years. The serrated 110mm blade is rounded at the end with a black (dishwasher-proof) nylon handle and each knife comes in an individual plastic sheath.

THREE-PIECE SET $20.00
This three-piece set includes a vegetable knife, a serrated knife (as described above) and a right-handed potato peeler with a matching black handle, presented in a white plastic wallet.

GIFT BOXED KNIFE SET $44.00
This set contains five knives plus a matching right-handed potato peeler. There is a straight bladed vegetable knife and a serrated knife (as above), as well as a handy 85mm serrated blade vegetable knife, a small (85mm) utility knife with a pointed tip and a smaller (85mm) serrated knife. These elegantly presented sets make ideal gifts.

SERRATED CARVING KNIFE $28.50
This fabulous knife cuts beautifully and is a pleasure to use, it's ideal for carving or cutting fresh bread. The 21cm serrated blade does not require sharpening. Once again the knife has a black moulded, dishwasher safe handle and comes in a plastic sheath.

COOK'S KNIFE $35.00
An excellent all-purpose kitchen knife. With a well balanced 19cm wedge-shaped blade and a contoured black nylon handle, these knives make short work of slicing and chopping, and have come out on top of their class in several comparative tests. Each dishwasher-safe knife comes with its own plastic sheath.

STEEL $20.00
These steels have a 20cm 'blade' and measure 33cm in total. With its matching black handle the steel is an ideal companion for your own knives, or as a gift. Alison gets excellent results using these steels. N.B. Not for use with serrated knives.

PROBUS SPREADER/SCRAPER $6.50
After her knives, these are the most used tools in Alison's kitchen! With a comfortable plastic handle, metal shank and flexible plastic blade (suitable for use on non-stick surfaces), these are excellent for mixing muffin batters, stirring and scraping bowls, spreading icings, turning pikelets etc., etc....

NON-STICK TEFLON LINERS
Re-usable SureBrand Teflon liners are another essential kitchen item – they really help avoid the frustration of stuck-on baking, roasting or frying. Once you've used them, you'll wonder how you did without!

Round tin liner
(for 15-23cm tins) $6.50
(for 23-30cm tins) $9.50

Square tin liner
(for 15-23cm tins) $6.50
(for 23-30cm tins) $9.50

Ring tin liner
(for 23cm tins) $6.95

Baking sheet liner
(33x44cm) $13.95

Prices as at 31 March 2003, all prices include GST. Please add $3.50 post & packing to any knife/spreader order (any number of items). Please note, Teflon prices include post & packing.

Make cheques payable to Alison Holst Mail Orders and post to: Alison Holst Mail Orders
FREEPOST 124807
PO Box 17016
Wellington

Or visit us at **www.holst.co.nz**